Embellishing
with
Anything

Fiber Art Techniques for Quilts—ATCs, Postcards, Wallhangings & More

Gladys Love

Cont

Text copyright © 2009 by Gladys Love

Artwork copyright © 2009 by C&T Publishing, Inc.

Publisher: Amy Marson

Creative Director: Gailen Runge

Editors: Maria Capp and Kesel Wilson

Technical Editors: Susan Nelsen and Nanette Zeller

Copyeditor/Proofreader: Wordfirm Inc.

Cover Designer: Christina Jarumay

Book Designer: Amy Gonzalez Daniel

Production Coordinator: Zinnia Heinzmann

Illustrator: Mary Flynn

Photography by Christina Carty-Francis and Diane Pedersen of C&T Publishing, Inc., unless otherwise noted.

Published by C&T Publishing, Inc., P.O. Box 1456, Lafayette, CA 94549

Library of Congress Cataloging-in-Publication Data

Love, Gladys

Embellishing with anything : fiber art techniques for quilts--ATCs, postcards, wallhangings & more / Gladys Love.

  p. cm.

  Summary: "Embellishing with Anything provides techniques, instruction, and ideas for creating artist trading cards, postcards, journal pages, and wall art"--Provided by publisher.

  ISBN 978-1-57120-588-9 (softcover : alk. paper)

  1. Textile crafts. I. Title.

  TT699.L69 2009

  746--dc22

                    2008037422

Printed in China

10 9 8 7 6 5 4 3 2 1

ents

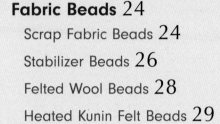

Dedication

Dedicated to the memory of Doreen Rennschmidt. Undaunted by artistic challenges large and small, she was a fearless and prolific creator who transitioned seamlessly among quilt arts, oil painting, and textiles. Her unwavering friendship and creative energy inspired and encouraged many of the women whose work appears in this book. She is profoundly missed.

Written by Ms. Marnie Rice

Acknowledgments

I must first tell my husband, Bob, just exactly how much I love and appreciate him for being so supportive. While I was busy with the book, he cooked, cleaned, did laundry, and walked the dog to allow me time to work. He has been wonderful and an indispensable support. I love you, Bob.

My lifetime friend and soul mate, Judy Bartel, kept me going with her encouragement and by working along with me on each project, trying out my instructions and creating her own pieces of art. Photographs of her work are included in each chapter. I can't imagine doing a project like this without you, Judy.

Other very special friends have helped me with their time. Joan Darling proofread for me, and I really appreciate her attention to detail. I also want to say how very much I appreciate the willing and enthusiastic participation of everyone who did something for this book. Thank you to all my friends for your encouragement and support. Thank you also to my sons, their wives, and my grandchildren for allowing me time off from my mother and grandmother duties to get this completed. I love that you understood.

I also need to thank Jan Grigsby of C&T Publishing for having faith in me and keeping my proposal alive while I went through a major move. All my supplies were put in storage for two months! It was all worth it, because now I have a great workspace and this book. Thank you, Jan, for getting me here.

My editors, Maria Capp and Kesel Wilson, have been wonderful to work with and incredibly helpful. I would also like to recognize Susan Nelsen for being so diligent in making sure everything made sense and making up for the technical part missing from my personality. They were all patient and helpful with me being a new writer. I have had a wonderful experience with C&T, and I actually look forward to doing it again!

Introduction

Question: What is an Artist Trading Card (ATC)?

Answer: An ATC is a small piece of artwork the size of a playing card, with a finished size of 2½″ × 3½″. ATCs cannot be bought or sold, only traded, thus their name. They provide wonderful gifts, keepsakes, souvenirs, or mementos. ATC groups are popping up all over the world, and exchange is happening on international as well as local levels. ATCs are easy to mail and special to receive. Trading these tiny art pieces can bring together people from all parts of the world.

A dear friend and fellow quilter, Doreen was recently diagnosed with cancer. Because of this, she couldn't attend an upcoming quilting retreat with a group we are lucky to be a part of. In a group discussion on how to let her know that she was missed, I proposed that we each make an ATC that represented ourselves. We could then send them to her, and she could guess who made which one.

Everyone joined in enthusiastically, making the project successful. The collection was *wonderfully* wide ranging in both technique and style, with *extremely* touching messages on the backs. She was thrilled with her "wee gifties." Her joy and enthusiasm in receiving these ATCs made me want to share this idea with any and all groups or individuals who might be interested. It also became the inspiration for this book. Amazing things can come in small packages!

ATCs are great fun because they provide an opportunity to play with techniques and unusual materials without committing huge sums of money, time, or supplies. It is so much fun to squelch that practical upbringing and melt, burn, glue, paint, dye, embellish, and stitch. It is also very rewarding to trade the results with friends, use them as gifts, or keep them as mementos of special occasions.

This book was written to provide instruction and ideas for creating ATCs, postcards, journal pages, and wall art. My hope is that you will learn to enjoy playing the ATC game and use these small projects as stepping stones to larger art quilts. If that happens just once, I will have successfully shared everything fiber art has done for me. Have fun and enjoy!

Gladys Love

Inspiration and Sketchbooks

Inspiration and creativity are strange phenomena. They can be with you, or they can be on hiatus and make you wonder if you'll ever have a good idea again. I'm definitely not a drawing specialist, but I have found a way to record thoughts, ideas, and general concepts so I can remember them.

Inspiration

Inspiration, with the right attitude and mind-set, can be found everywhere. It's not just in that glorious sunrise on the glacier over our valley—the sunrise that colors the snow pink and the ocean purple. It doesn't have to be the incredible sight of the cherry tree blooming in spring or the leaves turning color in the fall. It can be a previously unnoticed tree seen from a particular angle, a bulrush in the ditch, or a bird on a fence post. It can be a splat of paint on the laundry room floor, the way a dead tree fell over in the bush, a formation of driftwood on the beach, the arrangement of seaweed on the sand, or—very often for a textile artist—a piece of fabric.

My inspiration stems from my love of textiles, nature, people, artists I admire, and magazine photographs. I tear pictures out of magazines—and not just quilting or stitching magazines—and keep them in a scrapbook. I look at magazines on painting, photography, travel, and other topics. I don't cut out the pictures so that I can do exactly that image in fabrics; sometimes it's simply a combination of colors or an angle or some other tiny little detail that I like.

Creativity

Creativity is, to my mind, what we actually *do* with inspiration. The idea that comes from the initial seed of thought, how it is executed, and the colors and materials used *all* contribute to our own personal style in our work. It is that personal style that makes *your* work special.

Originality

Originality is another issue. Some people will copy your work. Although that is not OK, it is truly the greatest form of compliment. It is also important to consider the question of what originality actually is. On three occasions in my quilting life, I've dreamt up an idea, sketched it, dated it, started making it, and then found that all the way across the world somebody else had practically the same idea.

An example is the time I sketched out an idea, dated it, and began collecting fabrics. Practically the exact same quilt met the world on the cover of a new book. I hadn't started mine yet, and the other book was done! My local quilt shop owner really took a jab at me with this one. She sent the postcard from the publishers to me and on the back she wrote, "No more procrastinating, Gladys!"

Sketchbooks

In terms of where to start with inspiration, I feel it is important to have some kind of book of your ideas. A rough sketch of what you think might work, some scribbled notes along with it, and possibly a picture or two. I have found that if my idea journal or scrapbook is too "nice" (handmade paper and a beautiful cover), I hesitate to scribble and make notations in it. So I usually carry around a plain black spiral-bound sketchbook. With it, I feel confident in scribbling, doodling, writing notes, taping in pictures, and just getting all my ideas together in one place without having to make them beautiful.

Page from my sketchbook showing the birth of
Cherry Tree in Bloom Journal Cover, page 67

Supplies

See Resources, pages 95–96, for more information on these products and manufacturers.

Sewing machine

Any sewing machine with straight, zigzag, buttonhole, and a few decorative stitches will work for the projects in this book. It must also be possible to drop the feed dogs. You will need sewing machine needles sized 100/16 and 80/10, as well as a metallic needle.

Sewing machine feet

The projects in this book use a ¼" seam foot, a walking foot, an open-toe appliqué foot, and an open-toe embroidery foot (the latter has a little raised "tunnel" for the extra layers of thread to go through).

Another indispensable machine foot is known by several names: darning foot, embroidery foot, and free-motion quilting foot, to name a few. You will need this foot to do the free-motion stitching required in several projects.

An open-toe, free-motion foot gives the greatest visibility when stitching.

Rulers

An Omnigrid ruler with a minimum size of 6" × 12" will get you through all the projects that do not have a pattern provided. I also like to keep a 6" × 24" ruler handy.

Rotary cutter

I always have two rotary cutters on hand. One has a large blade and is reserved for fabric only. The other has the regular-sized blade and is used for cutting plastic, paper, soluble stabilizer, and all sorts of other blade-dulling materials.

Turning tools

Many items around the home can be used for turning. For example, a big plastic straw or a chopstick will work. If you will be doing a lot of turning, I enthusiastically suggest getting yourself a set of turning tubes.

Stuffing tools

Stuffing can also be done with a chopstick or a similar elongated, pointed object. But again, if you are going to be doing more than one project (how can you not?), I recommend purchasing a stuffing fork and a medium-sized hemostat. These are invaluable in

getting your stuffing into an item smoothly and *without frustration*.

Scissors

Like the rotary cutters, I have scissors for special functions. I have separate scissors for quilting cottons, scissors for polyesters or "unknown content" fabrics, scissors for snipping away threads, and scissors for paper or thin metal.

Needles and pins

These are standard hand-sewing supplies. My pin collection includes short and long, heavy and thin, glass and plastic heads. I keep them all in one container so they are readily available. I keep beading needles on hand, too.

Adhesives

I like to keep a UHU gluestick on my cutting table to grab easily while laying out projects. Gluesticks work very well and give off no fumes. Spray adhesives are also very handy, but do remember to use them in a well-ventilated area or step outside to spray your surface. I keep white glue and cans of basting spray handy, too.

Fray check

This handy product is great for keeping raw edges from fraying. Fray check *can* mark a surface though, so test it before using it on your finest quilt. However, for many of the design elements I make, such as trees and edges of leaves, this marking often adds to the random beauty of the objects.

Fixative spray

Fixative spray works to seal the surface and keep finished work from smudging or fading. A fixative also provides some protection from moisture, although it does not make the project "washable". It is especially nice to know the piece you've painstakingly colored to perfection is not going to be ruined while you bead it or attach other pieces to it. Fixative spray works well with pencils, crayons, paints, and even felt-tip markers.

I use the clear matte finish (transparent latex spray) made by Krylon. Even when using the low odor variety, be sure to work in a well-ventilated area with a face mask. See the manufacturer's directions for how to apply it to your work.

Double-sided fusible webbing

Have at least a yard of double-sided fusible webbing available. I use Steam-A-Seam 2. It won't be wasted and will be handy for when you get sudden artistic inspiration. Try to keep both lightweight and heavyweight on hand, as sometimes a heavier one with more adhesive is needed to keep thicker fabrics performing as you want them to.

Stabilizers

Many of the projects in this book use a very firm stabilizer as a working base. The ATCs and postcards are constructed in a "sandwich," just like a quilt, except that the inside layer is a heavy stabilizer. Some stabilizers are fusible, while others are not.

A very good fusible stabilizer is C&T Publishing's fast2fuse, which comes in different weights and has a fusible layer

on both sides. Use a pressing cloth underneath it when applying the first surface.

I also often use C&T Publishing's Timtex as a stabilizer. Timtex comes in several weights, but it does require the addition of fusible webbing. I keep a stash of precut pieces of Timtex in my studio for when inspiration hits suddenly. My most commonly used sizes are 2½″ × 3½″ for ATCs and 4″ × 6″ for postcards.

Soluble stabilizers

I used soluble plastic film stabilizers in several steps of my *Leaf Vine Luggage Tags*, page 79. I recommend that you have the following stabilizers on hand:

* Soluble Wash Away Avalon Ultra by Madeira

* Trace Away water-soluble stabilizer by H. A. Kidd and Company Limited

* Trans-Web paper-backed stabilizer by HTCW, Inc.

Quilter's Vinyl

One of the projects in this book is covered with a plastic layer to preserve the items underneath. C&T Publishing's Quilter's Vinyl is excellent for this, as it allows "pockets" that can be used to protect an embellishment, such as the dragonfly wings on page 63. Quilter's Vinyl can also be used to hold a loose item so that it can move around,

adding extra dimension to your artwork.

Tyvek

Tyvek is a non-woven, high-density polyethylene material. It can be purchased at stationery supply stores as large envelopes or from art supply stores in different size sheets.

Tyvek is practically impossible to tear but cuts like paper and is water resistant. It can be painted, stitched, and best of all, heated. Applying heat to the surface will cause it to bubble and distort, creating textured surfaces that can be sewn to another surface—but be sure to work in a well-ventilated area when applying heat.

Lutradur

Lutradur is a non-woven stabilizer available in several different weights. The lightest is somewhat translucent, and the heaviest is opaque. It can be heated, burned, painted, stitched, beaded, stamped, or any other surface embellishment technique you desire.

Because it is non-woven, it will not unravel, and it keeps a clean edge. Heavier weights work well as an ATC or journal page. The lighter weights are good for embellishments.

Embroidery hoop

For two of the projects in this book, you will need an embroidery hoop. This hoop should be 6″ or 8″ in circumference and should be able to move around in the throat of your machine without bumping into the body. I prefer wooden hoops because the fabric stays tighter than in plastic hoops. An extra bonus is finding a hoop shallow enough to fit under the free-motion foot.

Thread and embroidery floss

Lots and lots of thread and embroidery floss. More is more . . . whatever you can find . . . build your stash . . . never enough . . . try everything . . . it's never wasted. You can never have enough varieties of thread and embroidery floss!

Pressing cloths

Pressing cloths are absolutely necessary when using fusible stabilizers. A pressing cloth beneath your work will save the ironing board cover from messes, and one over the top of your work will save your precious iron.

Iron

My iron has a nice point on it, which I like for opening seams and pressing seams flat. It is also a steam iron, as I often use steam. You will need the iron for regular pressing, as well as for applying fusible webbing and for heat setting painted, printed, and stamped fabrics.

You should be using a pressing cloth (see above). However, if you do get fusible adhesive on your iron, keep the iron hot and rub it back and forth on an old towel. This usually removes the mess. *Do* remove the adhesive, because it is known to come off on the most precious object at the worst possible time.

Heat gun

A heat gun is needed for many of the projects in this book (a hair dryer won't do). I have both a crafter's heat gun and a builder's heat gun. I find the pistol shape of the builder's gun easier to use, but it is *very* hot, so be extra careful. The crafter's version is not as hot and may take a little longer, but you will avoid the tragedy of having your project melt into oblivion before your very eyes! The crafter's gun also has a smaller nozzle, making it easier to direct the heat to the desired area of your project.

Embellishments

Besides the obvious beads, buttons, and sequins, I collect embellishments at thrift stores by buying broken jewelry, clothing with fantastic buttons, hats with phenomenal feathers, or any other item that could add character to a design. I also collect bits and pieces from the beach, twigs and mosses from the yard, acorns and cones from walks in the woods, as well as odds and ends in parking lots.

I love to embellish with silk, so I often have silk rods, cocoons, and throwster's waste on hand to add another natural element. Decorative yarns and raw wool add a nice touch. Anything that looks good to you will probably find its way into your artwork. It's the same theory as fabric: If you buy what you like, even without a plan, it tends to come together nicely.

Fabric paints

I like to paint fabric in advance to have something unusual on hand when I want to make an ATC or a postcard. The finish on painted fabric creates a nice surface for rubber-stamped designs, which makes your work unique and original. I highly recommend Jacquard Lumiere and Setacolor by Pebeo brand paints.

Rubber stamps

A collection of rubber stamps with designs that appeal to you is perfect for decorating fabric. Natural themes like leaves, trees, and insects are good choices. Rubber stamps are often produced by "angel companies" which release the design copyright so that many people can use it in their art. In general, it's OK to use a rubber stamp in a design you are going to show or sell; however, like so many other things, it's wise to check first. All the producers of the stamps used in this book have given me permission to feature their items.

Computer and printer

The computer and printer are invaluable tools in today's textile arts. Although you don't have to be proficient at many different software programs, they can help when your handwriting isn't as decorative as you'd like or when you want a subtle addition to your artwork. I use this technology in many ways: to print a poem or thought for the day or to make a unique design for a special project.

Spray starch

Spray starch stiffens the fabric and gives a very clean-cut edge.

Now let's put this all together and get creative!

Techniques

The following techniques are used to make the projects featured in this book. Any of the projects can be made as an ATC, postcard, or wallhanging by adjusting the size of the foundation. Refer back to this section as needed.

Assembling the Sandwich

Each project is made up of three basic layers: a design surface, a middle material, and a backing fabric. This "sandwich" varies, depending on what material is used as the middle layer.

The design surface—the fabric you select as the background for your design—is the top layer of the sandwich.

For ATCs and postcards, the middle layer is a heavier form of stabilizer. C&T Publishing's fast2fuse is an excellent stabilizer, as is their Timtex. For wallhangings and larger projects, I use quilt batting as the middle layer. I prefer wool batting, as it is lightweight and gives the design layer a nice surface.

The backing of these projects varies. I have used everything from hand-painted fabric to purchased fabric. Sometimes I use home-decorating fabric, as it adds even more firmness to a project. I choose the backings on the spur of the moment. Sometimes I want the backing to coordinate with the front, while other times I use whatever is available. It all depends on personal taste.

Finishing the Edges

Several edge-finishing methods are used in the projects. I generally use a machine satin stitch, a decorative stitch preset on my machine, or a hand buttonhole stitch, sometimes with beads added.

Your machine likely has decorative stitches that will work. Look for stitches that are straight on one side and extend out for the decorative part. An example of this is the stitch used on the *Feathers, Bones, and Driftwood* project, page 19.

The machine satin stitch edge is the easiest edge finish to use. It fastens all three layers of the sandwich together, while also stabilizing design elements and embellishments. Machine satin stitching is done simply by setting your machine to a zigzag stitch wide enough to catch and cover all three layers and short enough that you can't see through it—in other words, a solid stitch that is approximately ¼˝ wide.

Machine Satin Stitching

1. Choose a suitable thread for the top thread *and* the bobbin, as they will both show. Thread your machine.

2. Set your machine to a zigzag stitch that is about ¼˝ wide and very close together (on my Pfaff, it's 3.0 wide and 0.25 length).

3. After testing the thread and stitch for appearance, start at a corner on your trimmed piece and work your way around the project, with the outside edge of the stitch going right off the edge of the card to seal in any raw edges. Stitch right to the edge of the first corner. Leave the needle down on the outside edge of the stitch. Lift the foot, carefully turn the project, and place it right against the needle. Lower the foot and proceed down the next edge. Continue in this manner along all 4 sides of the card.

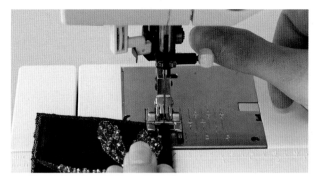

Stitch edge and turn corner.

4. When you reach the starting point, sew right off the edge. Lift the needle and the presser foot, releasing the tension on the thread. Pull your project out far enough to have about 10″ of thread and snip free of the machine.

5. Thread a needle and weave these ends into the zigzag stitch to finish.

thread preview tip

It is helpful to use some scrap fabric strips with a strip of stabilizer in a little sandwich as a practice run. This way you can test your threads and stitch size, giving you a preview of the finished edging stitch and allowing you to change your mind if a metallic or other decorative thread is not cooperating. Try a stitch width a bit narrower to see how you like it. Experiment!

Buttonhole Stitching by Hand

Buttonhole stitch done by hand

Beads added to buttonhole stitch done by hand

Pillowcase Finish

For wall art, I sometimes use a traditional binding, but most often I use what I call a pillowcase finish. *It is important to lay this sandwich in the correct order, so that when turned, the batting is inside the sandwich.* This edge finish completes the quilt without binding on the edge.

1. Cut the backing fabric and batting to *exactly* the same size as your trimmed design top.

2. Lay the batting on the table first. Then lay the embellished piece *right side up on top* of the batting. Place the backing on top with the *right side down*. Pin the edges, matching them all exactly. Ignore lumps that the embellishments may form; just make sure all 3 layers are perfectly even along the edges.

Layering for pillowcase finish

3. Backstitch 2 stitches, then stitch forward to start a ¼″ seam along one edge of the quilt sandwich about ⅓ from the middle. You may find it useful to use a walking foot if your machine has one. Stop with the needle down ¼″ from the corner of the backing fabric. Lift the presser foot and turn the work. Repeat this step around the entire rectangle, stopping on the first edge about ⅓ of the way in, leaving a center area open for turning. Backstitch 2 stitches to finish the seam securely.

4. Clip the 4 corners at an angle for a sharper corner after turning.

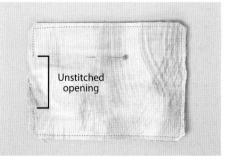

Unstitched opening

Clip corners before turning.

5. Reach inside through the opening and gently turn the project right side out.

6. Lay it flat and press the edges, making sure they are completely turned and the corners are fully opened.

7. Hand stitch the seamline closed.

corner tip

Use a chopstick from the inside to push out the seam while pressing to help ensure that the edges will be fully turned out and the corners square. This also helps avoid burning your fingers!

Cutting and Piecing Curved Seams

This technique can be used to create many interesting backgrounds for additional embellishment or appliqué. I use curved seam cutting and piecing to add dimension and variety to my backgrounds. In this technique, strips of fabric are sewn together to make irregular, curved seams. With a little practice, this technique is easy and rewarding. To make the curved seams lie flat, you must cut each piece so that the edges and curves match perfectly. The simplest way to do this is to overlap two pieces of fabric and cut both at the same time with a rotary cutter. If you've never done this before, it's best to try it on some scraps first.

1. With both fabrics face up, place Fabric B on top of Fabric A slightly toward the right, creating an overlap of the fabrics. Make sure there is enough overlap for the gentle curved line you are about to cut. The top edges should be even, as you will align these edges to sew the seam.

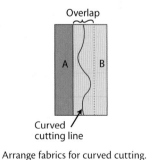

Arrange fabrics for curved cutting.

2. With the rotary cutter, cut a gentle curved line from edge to edge, within the area of your overlap.

curve cutting tip

It is wise to make these gentle curved cuts starting and ending in a straight line for ease of stitching, as doing so makes it much easier to start and end the seam.

3. Gently lift the discard Fabric B piece from the *left* of the cut line. To the *right* of the cut line and beneath Fabric B, there will be a Fabric A piece to discard. Sometimes these offcuts are wide enough to be used in another seam on the same piece.

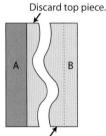

Remove discard pieces.

4. Layer Fabric B on top of Fabric A, right sides together. Carefully align the top edges of the cut.

Layer Fabric B over Fabric A, matching start of cut.

5. Set your machine to a straight stitch of standard length and engage the needle-down position, if your machine offers that option. Start the seam of the 2 cut curved pieces at the straight edge beginning of the cut. Sew ½" or so and arrange Fabric A so that it is flat on the sewing deck, with your right hand working as a guide. Hold up Fabric B in your left hand, remembering not to pull as you stitch. Guide the 2 edges together in a ¼" seam. (*Note:* I do not recommend pinning this seam because of the bias edges. The less it is handled the better it will fit.)

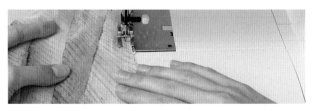

Guide gently with both hands while stitching.

6. When finished, clip the curves so that the seam will lay flat when pressed. The gentler your curves, the easier this step will be. It is not possible to keep all the edges even, so don't worry about that now.

7. Press the seam with a steam iron: Lay the piece flat, right side up, and run the tip of the iron along the seam, opening it with the iron as you go. This might be considered a controversial way to press, but pressing in this manner guarantees there will be no folded seams on your design surface. After pressing from the top, turn it over and press the back so the seam allowances all lie in the same direction. This will avoid unwanted lumps and bumps. Repeat the pressing from the front.

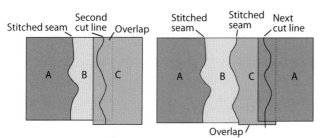

Press curved seam.

8. Repeat Steps 1–7 to add more strips to your background until it is the width you want. The top and bottom edges of the background panel are uneven, but these will be trimmed later.

Continue to add strips to the panel.

Finished background piece—Uneven top and bottom will be trimmed later.

one seam at a time tip

Work on one seam at a time. Curved seams distort with sewing and pressing. Therefore, you will avoid frustration by working one cut, seam, and pressing at a time. The finished product can be pressed and trimmed to size later.

Twin-Needle Top Stitching

This technique is born of an adventurous spirit. I had seen twin needles used in clothing construction but didn't like the straight geometric lines usually created. I purchased one twin needle for a test run and loved what it did to a fabric surface. The rest is history. This is one of the ways I use the twin needle.

1. Refer to your sewing machine instruction book to set up your machine with a twin needle and the proper foot. Use 2 threads of your choice to be seen on the top of the fabric. (*Note:* This top stitching will shrink the background piece anywhere from 2″ to 4″ in width, depending on how much stitching is done and on the width of the twin needle. I generally use a 6.0/100 needle.)

Use a twin needle that is compatible with your machine.

2. Fill at least 2 bobbins, as this technique uses a lot of bobbin thread. The good thing about this technique is that the bobbin thread doesn't show, so it doesn't have to be special thread.

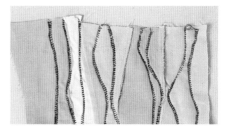

Back of top-stitched piece—Bobbin thread will be covered later by backing.

3. Start from an edge of the pieced background and stitch slowly from top to bottom, lifting both the twin needle and the foot to change directions. You can start again right there or move to either side to start the next line. Stitch with random wavy lines that touch and then move away from each other. There is no need to follow the seamlines, as topstitching in this manner is designed to add texture and variety. You can topstitch over the seamline without difficulty—just exercise common sense with your speed.

variety of curves tip

When cutting gentle curves, keep an eye on the previous seam and vary the shape to enhance the piece. Try not to repeat the same curved line to avoid the look of stripes.

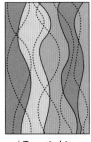

⌇ Top stitching

Seamlines and stitch lines add texture to background.

4. Press the top-stitched background with a steam iron to push the ridges one way or another, or just press randomly and let them fall where they may. I haven't noticed an appreciable difference in the outcome whichever way it gets pressed, but it does need to be pressed. (*Note:* The background is still uneven at this point; it will be cut to size in a later step.)

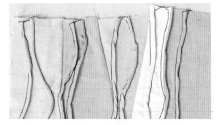

Finished curved background (high-contrast thread used for illustration purposes)—Notice the possible effects when using two thread colors.

machine tension tip

Before you begin, do a test of this stitch on a scrap of the fabric you plan to use. Depending on the weight of your fabric, it is sometimes necessary to adjust your top and bobbin tension so that the ridge forms properly to your satisfaction. Incorrect tension makes two stitch lines side by side or an undesirable pucker. *Loosening the top tension* and *tightening the bobbin* by a quarter turn to the right on the bobbin case screw will pull the fabric into a ridge as required.

quilting gloves tip

I wear quilting gloves to hold the piece flat as I feed it through the machine.

Double-Fused Fabrics

This is a technique I came up with that was inspired by a model on the cover of a magazine. She was wearing a vest that was absolutely stunning, with a spray of leaves down the front. The leaves were intriguing, and I wanted to find a way to duplicate them. After a little experimentation, this is what I came up with. Double-fused fabrics are used in the *Ginkgo Leaves Wallhanging*, page 52, and the *Red Dragonfly Wallhanging*, page 57.

1. Cut 2 pieces of fabric and a piece of double-sided fusible webbing to the same size. I prefer a heavyweight webbing, as I do not want floppy elements. I find the new lightweight materials too fine for this use.

2. Place a pressing cloth on your ironing surface (or use an old clean tea towel). Place a piece of fabric *right side down* on the pressing cloth. Remove the paper from both sides of the webbing and layer the webbing on the fabric. Layer the second piece of fabric *right side up* on top of the webbing. Cover with a second pressing cloth and press according to the manufacturer's directions. The time required for pressing depends in part on the fabrics used.

Layering for double-fused fabric

tip

A fused fabric section can be used to create project elements, such as this curling leaf.

Sample leaf—Note natural curling on the stem.

Couching with Decorative Threads

I have used a variety of threads for couching, including embroidery threads, several varieties of "exotic" knitting yarns, and thin metal wire. One of the best ways to have a collection of suitable strands for couching is to purchase the packages that come with approximately 1 yard of several threads combined (Oliver Twists is a good example). That way you get a variety of threads in the color range for your particular project. If you are a knitter, you will have leftovers that are perfect for these little projects.

1. Use a chalk pencil to draw the design lines on the item you are about to decorate. Thread selection is your choice. (*Note:* For the turned ginkgo leaf in the *Ginkgo Leaves Wallhanging*, page 52, I used a matching thread so that the couched strand became the feature of focus.) The bobbin thread should be either complementary or invisible, as it will show on the opposite side of the three-dimensional leaf. Guide the fabric under an open-toe embroidery foot and lay thread down on the drawn lines. Stitch slowly with a zigzag stitch to fasten the thread in place.

2. Stitch from the top of the stem to an outside edge. At the edge, stop with the needle down, lift the foot, turn the leaf, and proceed to couch decorative threads along the edge to the next line. Repeat this sequence to stitch from the bottom of the leaf back up the stem.

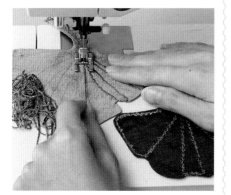

Couch decorative strand to turned leaf.

3. When finished, take the strand and stitching to the top of the stem and snip there. Seal the stem with fray

check so nothing unravels. These stems will be curled, which hides the tip.

Turned Pieces with Small Openings

One of the repeated elements in this book is an embellishment made by turning two layers sewn together (see the *Ginkgo Leaves Wallhanging*, page 52, for a turned ginkgo leaf, and the *Beaded Goddess Postcards*, on page 36).

1. Trace the desired pattern onto freezer paper and cut out.

2. Place 2 fabrics right sides together and press the template into place. Pin the fabric layers together, if needed.

3. Set your machine to a very tiny stitch (on my Pfaff, I use 1.0). Sew around the template, just outside the template edge. Use an open-toe foot on your machine so you can see clearly as you stitch. Keep the needle in the needle-down position for turning at the curves and leave an opening (as indicated on the pattern) for turning.

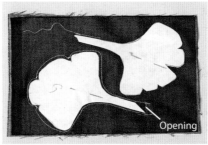

Sew around template.

4. When stitching inside curves, do 2 or 3 stitches at the top of the curve, backstitch, and stitch again before proceeding down the other side. This provides space to clip a sharp curve

or point. Mastering this step will allow you to turn pointed leaves and the arms and legs of dolls with ease.

Backstitch on inside curves.

5. Cut out your shape. Clip the seam allowance every ¼" along the curves and inside points to facilitate smooth turning.

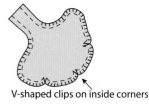

V-shaped clips on inside corners

Clip every ¼".

6. Gather your turning tools. The easiest way to turn any small item is to use a tube and a blunt-ended instrument. Use a smooth but firm plastic or metal tube that fits into the opening. You also need a straight stick of wood or wire with a very smooth end that can fit into the tube with a little room to spare. The wire or wood shouldn't be so sharp that it pokes through the fabric. I have successfully used both a drinking straw and a chopstick as a turning tool.

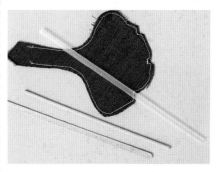

Turning tools

7. Put the turning tube into the opening. Push the tube to the opposite seam and hold it there with one hand. With your other hand, push the stick on the seam allowance (to allow less chance of it poking through your fabric) and push it up into the tube as far as it will go without forcing.

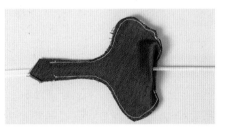

Insert tube all the way to opposite seam and push stick and fabric into tube.

turning tools tip

If you intend to do much turning, I strongly recommend purchasing Patti Culea's Itsy Bitsy Finger Turner turning tube set and Barbara Willis's Stuffing Fork—both of which are indispensable for projects like these (see Resources, page 95).

8. Remove the tube. I brace the stick against my stomach and use both hands to gently work the fabric down the stick (wet fingertips help). The right side will work its way out of the opening. At that point, you can remove the stick and use your hands to hold the edge showing through the opening and pull against the fabric, working the item down and right side out.

9. Pull gently so that you don't pop the seamline. When it's completely right side out, use the stick to push inside against the seams to get it completely turned, showing its full shape.

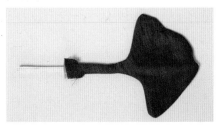

Fully turned leaf

10. Press the item. It's ready to use!

Raw-Edge Appliqué

Raw-edge appliqué is the simplest method of applying a fabric motif to a fabric surface. The motif is simply laid in place. You then use your sewing machine, with a free-motion foot attached, to straight stitch around the outline, as close to the edge as possible. The fabric edge is left unfinished (raw). This raw edge and the stitching contribute to the project's appearance. For an example, see *Blossoms a la Mucha Collage*, page 85.

Beading

Projects in this book are often embellished with seed beads. These beads are applied in the simplest way possible—by hand with a stab stitch. In a couple of projects, a line of beads is *couched* into place.

1. Choose a thread to match the bead. Knot the thread and come up with the needle from the back of the project (usually before the backing fabric is applied).

2. Pick up a bead with the needle and poke the needle down through the surface in the same spot, leaving a bead to decorate that spot.

3. Cover the crisscrossed threads on the back of your work by attaching the backing to the project.

For areas where I want heavy beading, like the circle around flowers or the tail of a dragonfly, I put more beads on the thread, lay them in place, and then couch the line of thread in place. Repeating this step quickly fills an area.

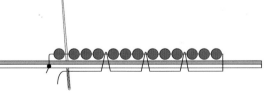

Couch line of beads to surface.

ephemera from Everywhere

Using findings and nonfabric items

Have you ever read those emails that analyze your personality by the way you walk? They ask, "Do you walk with your head up looking the world in the face?" or "Do you walk quickly looking left and right and not really noticing anything?" or "Do you walk slowly looking down at the ground?" Well, I used to walk fast and look the world in the face, for whatever that was worth, but since discovering the fun of making art out of found objects, my walking style, if not my personality, has certainly changed!

I walk on the beach and find pebbles, bits of fiberglass from a wrecked boat, brightly colored strands of rope, bits of driftwood, sun-bleached twigs, bleached bones, shells, and—my favorite—tumbled glass. I walk in the woods and find twigs, dried leaf skeletons, beautiful mosses, pebbles, feathers, tufts of fur, and sometimes an antler shed by a deer.

At sites where old buildings are being demolished, I find crushed bottle caps, rusted washers, splinters of painted wood, worn leather, pretty pieces of glass, and odd things that I can't identify but that will definitely find a place in my art someday. There's also broken jewelry to be had at the thrift shop, odds and ends at garage sales, and—the favorite of many—buttons and beads that have no home.

You can even find interesting objects in your home. The assortment of wine labels today can be an unending source of inspiration. My sister-in-law brings wine chosen for the label rather than the wine itself because she knows I'm going to make something out of it. I keep all those scratchy labels cut off the back of sweaters because they will make a nice collage. Foil bags can be melted, and sushi wrapping can make grass. It's never ending!

It's become impossible for me to walk anywhere without pockets or a little bucket or a bag to put my found goodies in. Here are some fun examples of how I have used findings in my work. I hope they inspire you to fill your pockets with found objects and incorporate them in your art.

Dancing Wine Label

This postcard was made from a wine label that my sister-in-law brought to a barbecue. She chose it especially for the label, which is a three-dimensional plastic in which people appear to be dancing when you move it. I loved it and went back for more of that wine . . . for the label, of course!

1. Use a gluestick to apply background fabric to a precut piece of 4″ × 6″ Timtex.

2. Cut the label into pieces and stitch scraps of trim around the edges to attach to the Timtex.

3. Use a gluestick to secure the backing to the other side and finish the edge with a satin stitch.

4. Add a fringe of dingle balls (a decorative stitch on many machines) across the top.

Scratch-No-More Clothing Labels

I save labels snipped out of my sweaters or my husband's new shirts. Some are quite unique and make a wonderful decoration for collage on an ATC or postcard. I'm hoping for the day when all of mine say M instead of XL—but still, they are fun to work with.

1. Use a gluestick to apply hand-painted cotton to a precut piece of 4″ × 6″ Timtex.

2. Arrange the labels on the surface of the cotton. When you are satisfied with the appearance, pin the labels into place.

3. Use a straight stitch to stitch each label into place.

4. Glue the backing to the other side and finish the edges with a decorative edge stitch.

Feathers, Bones, and Driftwood

Most of these bits came from the beach. Who knows what creature they belonged to at one time, but after tossing in salt water and being bleached in the sun, they have a certain appeal to a beachcomber like me. Again, the ATC is a great medium for displaying these odds and ends in an artistic way.

1. Cut hand-dyed fabric to size. Using a gluestick, attach it to a precut piece of 2½" × 3½" Timtex.

2. Use an awl to make a small hole in the driftwood. Stitch the driftwood into place through this hole.

3. Use a long needle to thread invisible thread through a little bone or other embellishment piece.

4. Slip a feather underneath the driftwood and bone.

5. Add some "pearls" (from a broken bracelet) and seed beads. (The little silver "wing" in this project is an earring that was a solo in the junk bowl at the school where I work.)

6. Glue the backing to the other side and finish with a decorative edge stitch.

Note: Keep in mind there are federal restrictions on owning or mailing certain feathers. Before you use or mail any such item, make yourself familiar with the law.

Frog Wine Label

I have been collecting frogs for years. It seems the best years with my boys were the ones in which we were hatching tadpoles and chasing frogs around their bedrooms. This wine label has a frog with attitude, and I couldn't resist adding him to my collection of personal ATCs. The label was easy to peel off the bottle and stick to a piece of saran wrap until I was ready to play with it.

1. Choose a suitable fabric print. Use your gluestick to attach it to a precut 2½" × 3½" Timtex card.

2. Cut around the interesting parts of your label. (I cut the frog part into the rough shape of a wine glass.) Stitch the cut pieces to the fabric/Timtex layer.

3. Add something silly, like a frog button, to contrast with the attitude.

4. Back with a scrap of muslin and finish the edges with a simple satin stitch.

Sushi Wrap

My best friend Judy clowns around and imitates Miss Piggy when she is asked to do something she doesn't want to do. Her favorite saying is, "Get yourself another pig." I made this ATC for her, using sushi wrap for the grass, and was lucky enough to find a cute pig button to finish it off.

1. Spray baste or gluestick fabric to a 2½″ × 3½″ piece of Timtex.

2. Program a fun expression into your sewing machine (practice on a scrap first) and stitch the writing onto the card.

3. Sew up and down the sushi-wrap grass to attach it.

4. Stitch a fun embellishment, like the pig button, into place.

5. Apply backing fabric and finish the edges with a satin stitch.

Candy Wrappers

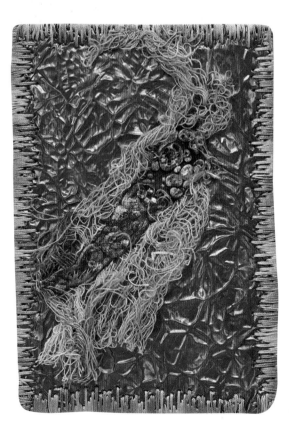

Candy wrappers come in the most delicious colors and are usually made of plastic that is sensitive to heat. I learned to do this technique in a class with Eileen Neill, who is also my bead source. When my granddaughters saw this piece, they started saving their brightly colored candy wrappers for me.

1. Pin a plastic candy wrapper to a cork tile and heat gently with a heat gun.

2. Using a gluestick, attach the crinkled wrapper to a 2½″ × 3½″ piece of Timtex.

3. Place a scrap of painted cheesecloth on top. On top of that, place a scrap of painted and melted Tyvek. Add a few beads to finish it off.

4. Glue the backing to the other side and finish the edge with a machine stitch.

Beer Can Calendar Girls

I found a whole bunch of beer cans left on the beach by some forgetful people. I was actually thrilled to pick up after them because each can had a different calendar girl on it. I've made a series from these. I used a heavy pair of paper scissors to trim the cans to shape, and the rest is history! What a great find. This postcard was fun to make.

1. Spray baste satin onto a precut piece of 4″ × 6″ Timtex.

2. Use a heavy pair of paper scissors to trim out interesting portions of the beer can. Use a gluestick to hold the cut pieces in place.

3. Add feathers or other fun elements that go with your theme.

4. Machine stitch the beer can pieces to the card with regular quilting thread and a denim needle, catching the embellishments where they pass under the metal (you will have to discard your needle afterward).

5. Add other embellishments, such as a clothing label, at the center.

6. Optional: Print a verse onto the backing fabric with your computer. Apply the printed backing with a gluestick and finish the edges with a machine satin stitch.

Birch Bark, Leather, and Fabric Beads

This card was made with birch bark that was peeling off the tree. I couldn't walk past the tree in the park and not collect the bark. The bark makes a beautiful background for this ATC, giving it a specific Western flair. The circle of leather is a discard from a tag on a new purse. The fabric beads were a gift from Judy Bartel.

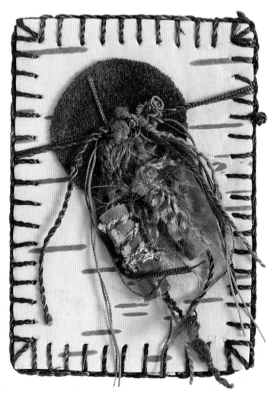

1. Using a gluestick, glue a piece of bark to a precut piece of 2½″ × 3½″ Timtex.

2. Use the gluestick to hold a leather piece in place (I used a circle of leather). With an awl, poke a hole in the center of the leather and then through the bark and the Timtex.

3. Wrap strands of decorative yarn around each side of the card, with the ends coming to the front through the hole in the leather. Tie the threads in a simple knot.

4. Add handmade beads with feather trim to the threads hanging from the knot and glue to the center of the leather with a dot of white glue.

5. Apply backing fabric. Use a bodkin with embroidery floss to work the buttonhole stitch border by hand.

Thrift Store Jewelry

My husband's favorite place to shop is a store called Value Village—a huge thrift shop. While he is scrounging for coveralls, blue jeans, and usable tools, I look for weird jewelry, fur collars, hats with unique embellishments, and bits of lace. Sometimes I'm really lucky. This card is made with some of my finds on one of those shopping trips.

1. Use a rubber stamp with pink-gold Lumiere paint to apply a face on plain muslin. When it is dry, heat set the paint. Use a gluestick to attach the muslin to a 2½″ × 3½″ piece of Timtex.

2. Drape broken necklaces over the head and stitch them down with invisible thread. Don't stitch right to the edge until after the backing is applied.

3. Add a backing and finish the edge with a satin stitch.

4. Stitch the jewels down right to the edge. (The "earring" on my piece was an expandable ring in its first life. I had my husband cut off the band, and then I used a long, bent beading needle to apply it to the ATC.)

5. Use pencil crayons to give the face more detail and spray it with a clear fixative.

Chinese Coins

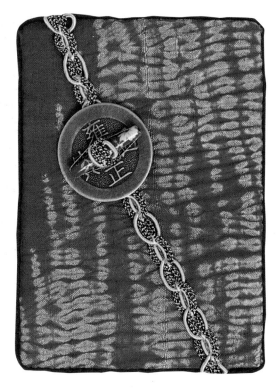

My friend Judy and I have been exchanging ATCs for almost two years now. We make two of each design, keeping one for ourselves and giving one to the other. This is great fun and keeps us thinking of small inspirational projects to enhance our collection. This is one I made for Judy during that exchange.

1. Using double-sided fusible webbing, fuse the backing fabric—in this case, a scrap of kimono silk, 3½″ × 4½″—to a piece of 2½″ × 3½″ Timtex, centering the Timtex.

2. Fold a short scrap of black-and-gold braid in half and push the fold up through the hole in the coin.

3. To secure the coin, place a long, skinny Oriental bead in the loop of the braid and tighten the braid so it will fit smoothly against the coin. The length of the bead will prevent the braid from sliding through.

4. Lay the strip of braid with the coin and bead diagonally across the surface of the ATC.

5. Machine stitch the braid with invisible thread on both sides, skipping over the coin.

6. Apply a hand stitch of invisible thread through the bead and down through the backing to keep the bead from sliding out (like sewing on a button).

7. Wrap the edges of the kimono silk around the Timtex stabilizer and use a gluestick to hold down the edges in the back. Glue this surface to a slightly larger square of wool felt to give it a very narrow, dark red border as a frame. Sew a label onto the felt before gluing the layers together so there is a good surface for signing.

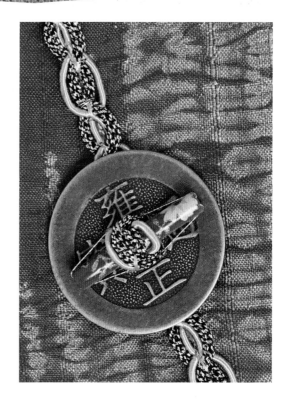

Dragonfly Skeleton

I found a dragonfly skeleton in the grass in my backyard. It was fascinating in its delicate and intricate design. It was so fragile, and yet I wanted to make this ATC with it. I did that by eliminating the body shell and just using the wings.

I gave this card to my friend Judy because she loves dragonflies. She was **so** pleased with it. Two weeks later, she got out of the car and discovered a skeleton just like the one I'd found lying in the grass. So not to be outdone, she made one for me, too!

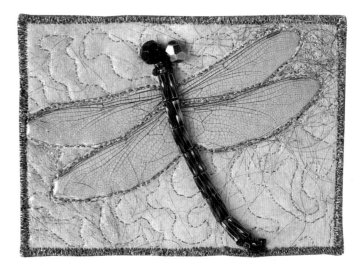

1. Glue or spray baste fabric onto a 2½″ × 3½″ piece of Timtex. Gently place the fragile wings onto the fabric.

2. Place a 2½″ × 3½″ piece of Quilter's Vinyl (see Resources, page 95) over the dragonfly and very carefully stitch around the outline of the wings.

3. Bead the center area to form the body.

4. Apply backing and finish the edges with a satin stitch.

fabric Beads

Rolled, felted, glued, and melted fiber beads

Fabric beads make great embellishments. For examples of how I have used them in projects, see **Red Dragonfly Wallhanging**, page 57, and **The Lady with the Blues Wallhanging**, page 74. I have three favorite (and not-too-messy) methods of making beads, each of which allows for lots of variety.

Scrap Fabric Beads

The first method uses fabric scraps. All those lovely little offcuts from other projects that we keep because they are too luscious to toss out suddenly offer themselves up for reconsideration. I have used silks, cotton lamés, cotton, and even polyesters. It's a very simple method that takes overnight to dry. The finished product is a lightweight and unusual addition to your collection of embellishments.

supplies

* **Fabric scraps, 1″ × 1″ square or larger**
* **White tacky glue, 1 tablespoon in a disposable container**
* **Water**
* **Paintbrush**
* **Bamboo skewer or knitting needle**
* **Plastic wrap**
* **Straight pins**
* **Pebeo opaque paint (water-based)**
* **Sparkly threads, decorative yarns, and eyelash wools**
* **Various beads and buttons**

Variety of finished scrap beads

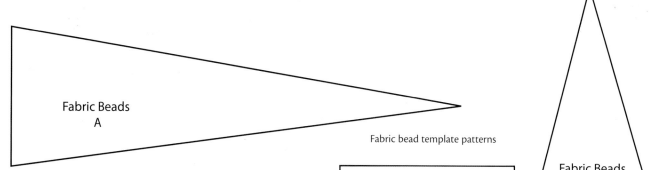

Fabric Beads
A

Fabric bead template patterns

Fabric Beads
B

Fabric Beads
C

instructions

1. Gather your supplies so you have everything on hand when you begin gluing.

2. Using the fabric bead template patterns as guides, cut fabric scraps into rectangles or triangles. Rectangles will give a smooth bead, whereas triangles will give barrel-shaped beads. The longer the triangle, the more layers in the middle, and thus the thicker the bead is around its tummy.

Scrap fabrics for beads; some can be used without trimming.

3. Cover the work surface with a protective cover or tape a piece of plastic wrap onto the work surface.

4. Wrap the bamboo skewer or knitting needle with plastic wrap to prevent the fabric from sticking to the surface.

5. Add 1 teaspoon of water to 1 tablespoon of glue and mix well.

6. Place a scrap of fabric on the work surface and paint the fabric with the glue mixture until it's saturated.

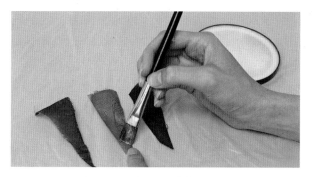

Paint scrap with watered-down glue.

7. Wrap this glue-soaked piece around the covered skewer or needle, starting with the wide end and wrapping right to the tip. Sometimes a fragile material frays a bit in the rolling process. Do not try to glue down these frayed threads, as they can add to the bead's interesting appearance.

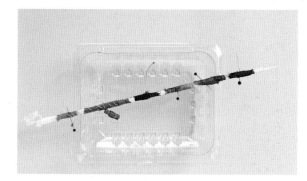

Roll glued fabric onto skewer.

8. Stick a pin in the tip to hold it in place and set it aside to dry overnight.

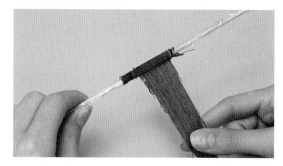

Wrap around bamboo skewer, pin, and set aside to dry.

9. After a night of drying, remove the pin and slide the bead off the skewer or needle.

Several beads can be wrapped around the same form and set aside to dry.

10. Embellish the beads. Here are some fun ideas:

* Wrap with metallic thread and small beads.

* Tie it like a tiny scroll with decorative yarns.

* Paint a different color. (If your paint is water based, leave the pin in place and paint sparingly, as it will loosen the glue. It's a good idea to stitch the bead closed before painting. If not stitched, let it dry again before removing the pin.)

* Wrap with fine wire with beads added here and there.

Arbutus Twigs ATC, 2½″ × 3⅓″, made by Judy Bartel, with rolled scrap beads.

Stabilizer Beads

These beads offer a good variety because you can make them in colors and fabrics that will match the project for which they are intended. They are a nice hand-stitching project and easy to make during your favorite TV show.

Finished stabilizer beads with various embellishments

supplies

* **Fine interfacing or stabilizer, 8½″ × 11″ (I used Lutradur in these samples.)**

* **Double-sided fusible webbing, 8½″ × 11″**

* **Organza, 8½″ × 11″**

* **Pebeo opaque paint (water-based)**

* **Paintbrush or sponge applicator**

* **Snippets of thread collected from other projects**

* **Decorative threads for machine**

* **Plain thread for bobbin**

* **Wooden bamboo skewer or knitting needle**

* **2 pressing cloths**

instructions

The fun of these beads is that you can make them the color you want or even use a combination of colors.

1. Pin the stabilizer to a work surface so it doesn't move around.

2. Paint the stabilizer liberally with whatever color or mixture of colors you like. Let dry overnight.

3. On a pressing cloth, press the painted stabilizer to flatten it. Remove the paper from one side of the fusible webbing and line up the sticky side on top of the painted stabilizer. With a pressing cloth underneath and the release paper on top, press to adhere the fusible webbing to the painted stabilizer.

4. Remove the top layer of paper. Sprinkle bits of thread all over the sticky surface, spreading them out evenly. These can be all the same color or mixed colors. A few tiny pieces of silk fabric or wool strands can also be added at this stage. Be sure to leave enough adhesive showing to allow the organza to adhere in the next step.

5. Place the chosen piece of organza on top of the snippets. With a pressing cloth underneath and on top, press firmly to fuse the organza.

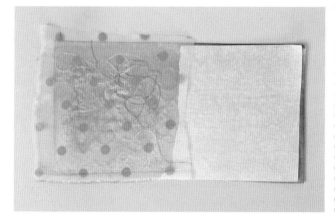

Textile base—Left half is ready to stitch on, right half still has paper backing and will be used to create a different-colored piece.

6. With your sewing machine, apply decorative stitching over the entire surface of the pressed thread sandwich. In a later step, you will cut this into smaller bits, so try to cover a good percentage of the surface with either stippling or lines of some kind. You can also change thread colors on one section so the finished beads have variety.

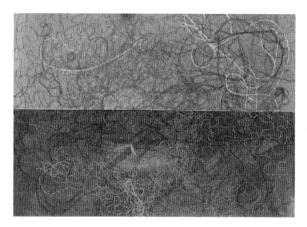

Stitch layers with more than one color of thread.

7. Cut strips 1¼″ wide from the sandwich and trim the ends straight.

8. Cut the strips into 2″-long pieces. These pieces will be rolled into beads.

Cut strips and pieces.

9. Roll each 2″ section onto a skewer or knitting needle.

10. Stick a pin into the bead to hold it in place. At this point, you can hold the bead on the skewer and hand stitch to secure the ends in place. Or you can wrap decorative thread around the middle 2 or 3 times, tie a double knot, and snip the ends to produce a little scroll.

Felted Wool Beads

Felting is one of the latest trends in creating and embellishing. It is simple to do and can produce wonderful results. Here is a way to make little round beads out of wool and then embellish them for your next project. These beads are unique because they can be sewn onto a surface or dangled on a strand. They have no actual hole, so they can be adjusted to whatever use you have in mind.

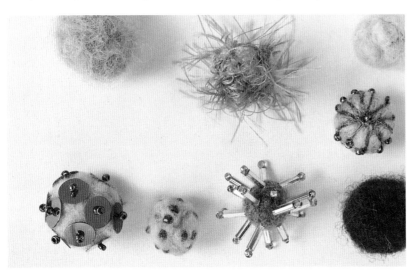

Felted beads

supplies

* **Small bits of washed raw wool, either plain or dyed colors**
* **Thick, tight-grain upholstery foam, 6″ × 6″**
* **Chopstick**
* **Hand-felting needle**
* **Variety of beads and sequins**
* **Decorative threads and yarns**

instructions

1. Take a pinch or curl of raw wool. (It's difficult to describe how much you need. You will know if you need more. Because it's easier to make your bead bigger than it is to make it smaller, start with less than you think you'll need.) Pull the wool apart a bit so it's fluffy.

Fluff wool for folding and felting.

2. Fold the wool fiber into itself as if you were folding a little towel. Continue doing this until you have a springy little bunch between your fingers.

3. Place the folded, rolled wool on the foam surface. Hold it in place with the chopstick.

Place folded wool fiber on foam for needle felting.

4. Repeatedly poke into the wool with the felting needle. You will quickly notice how the fibers begin to hold themselves in place and are not as springy.

5. Use the chopstick to free the fiber from the foam and roll it over. Continue poking with the felting needle while holding it down with the chopstick. Repeat this action until the ball is much smaller and tighter. If you wish to make it bigger, wrap the ball again with loose wool and repeat the stabbing until the outside layer is blended with the inside one.

safety tip

Danger! Hand-felting needles are very sharp and can cause you to bleed on your project if you don't pay very close attention. Use with extreme caution!

6. When the ball is finished, roll it under the palm of your hand against the foam surface. This rounds it out and blends the surface fibers so they are smoother.

7. Embellish with threads, yarns, beads, and sequins.

leftover paint tip

I often make these little felt balls in white and set them aside on my painting table. When I am done painting another project, I wet the woolen beads and pour leftover paint over them. This uses leftover paint that would otherwise be discarded, while also providing a variety of colored beads.

Plain white felted beads and beads soaked with leftover paints

Heated Kunin Felt Beads

My friend Judy Bartel makes the most wonderful beads from Kunin felt, a polyester-based, rather than wool-based, felt. She has agreed to share what she does. When Kunin felt is zapped with a heat gun, it gets tiny holes and creates great texture. This material also allows stitching on the felt before treating, much like the stabilizer beads on page 26. When they are done, these beads are a very satisfactory surface for paints and embossing powders. Kunin felt beads become hard after heat treatment.

Finished Kunin beads

supplies

* **Kunin felt, 1 piece 9″ × 12″, color of your choice (These are usually sold precut.)**
* **Knitting needle or bamboo skewer**
* **Old leather glove to protect hand**
* **Heat gun**
* **Straight pins**
* **Acrylic paints**
* **Embossing powder**

instructions

When heat treating any fiber, be sure you are in a well-ventilated room or outside.

1. Cut the felt into rectangles or triangles. Refer to the templates on page 25.

2. Wrap these cut pieces around a very thin knitting needle or bamboo skewer. Pin the overlap closed with a straight pin.

Roll Kunin triangles on skewer and pin in place.

3. Use a heat gun to zap the overlap first, just until it starts to melt. Remove the heat and press the overlap closed with a gloved fingertip. Continue to zap and press until you are happy with the texture.

Cream-colored felt looks like old eroding bones. A lower temperature craft heat gun was used.

embossing powders tip

Embossing powders can be purchased at scrapbooking supply stores. Apply paint or an acrylic medium to your bead, sprinkle it with the embossing powder, and heat again. The powder will bubble and thicken, giving a new texture to the bead surface. Embossing powders come in a variety of colors.

Paint Kunin felt beads, sprinkle with ultrathick embossing enamel, and heat again to give a metallic look.

caution

Wear a glove on the hand holding the skewer, especially if you are using a knitting needle. Even if you are using a bamboo skewer, the heat from the gun can sometimes cause discomfort—especially if you are really concentrating on the bead and forget where your fingers are.

 Tyvek tip

Tyvek can be used to embellish these beads. This unique material is very popular for projects like this, because it curls and bubbles when it melts. A good source of Tyvek is your local stationery store. Tyvek envelopes are a perfect size for these projects. Again, when working with heat and Tyvek, work outside or in a very well-ventilated area.

Kunin beads made with Kunin felt and machine-stitched designs topped with strips of painted and melted Tyvek.

tip

This same melting technique can be used with polyester organza. Organza scraps or strips are wrapped around the knitting needle in the same way, pinned in place, and heated. Organza will melt much more quickly and with much less heat. With a little practice, working with organza in this way can produce delightful, delicate trimmings for a special project.

Heat-treated organza beads

beaded print ATC

Sandwich assembly, free-motion stitching, beading, and satin stitching

Beaded print dragonfly ATC, 2½″ × 3½″, beaded in two color choices.

Dorothy, a long-time friend of mine, was the inspiration for this first project. We've been quilting together for at least 10 years now, and Dorothy is in her 80s. For one quilt, four very special friends and I arranged a round robin in which we all added different borders to the others' central block, resulting in a lap-size quilt.

Each border was themed. The first one had to be squares, the next triangles, the next appliqué, the next rectangles, and so on. Dorothy's contribution to each one was beautiful and **simple**. She added borders in plain fabric to the one requiring rectangles. For the border needing triangles, where we all tried to show off our piecing prowess, Dorothy added a big triangle to each side, effectively turning the central block on point. I have never forgotten the elegant simplicity she added to each quilt. Keeping in mind that theme of simplicity, here is a really simple ATC to get you started and your creative confidence flowing.

In this project, your fabric is doing the work for you, and you are simply adding to the statement that the fabric makes with your embellishments. The supply list is not "measured," as it is really up to you how much you add. Just play and have fun.

Various fabrics and the ATCs they produce—It's interesting to note that even a boring fabric can become a fabulous ATC.

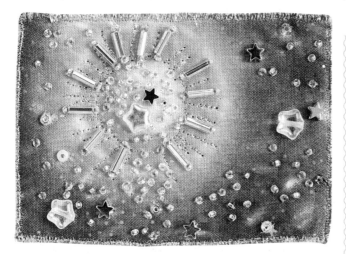

Supplies

* **Novelty print, fat quarter (You will be fussy cutting the part of the design that appeals to you most.)**

* **Backing fabric, 2½″ × 3½″ piece for each ATC you plan to make**

* **Heavyweight stabilizer, 2½″ × 3½″ for each ATC you plan to make (I use Timtex or fast2fuse.)**

* **Cardboard viewing frame with 2½″ × 3½″ opening (see Tip, page 33)**

* **Decorative sewing machine threads**

* **Various seed beads**

* **Beading needle to fit beads**

* **Colored pencils to contrast with the fabric**

* **Spray adhesive or fabric gluestick**

* **Invisible thread for your bobbin**

* **Free-motion foot**

making extras tip

Sometimes I make two or three ATCs at a time. By doing this, there's always one to keep and others to trade. I've never had all three turn out exactly the same, so they are all originals!

Sample fabric choices

Instructions

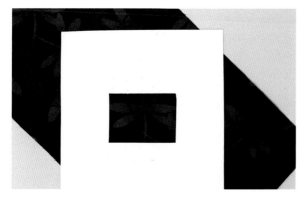

Use viewing frame to choose motif.

Choosing the Feature Print

1. Place the viewing frame over the motif in the fabric that appeals to you. Use the inner frame to draw a 2½″ × 3½″ rectangle around the chosen motif. (In the sample, I chose a dragonfly. Other fabric samples show different design possibilities.) Use a colored pencil that contrasts with the fabric so that it will show clearly.

Outline the rectangle.

2. Cut out the chosen rectangle right on the pencil lines. Use spray baste or a fabric gluestick to adhere the feature fabric to a 2½″ × 3½″ piece of stabilizer.

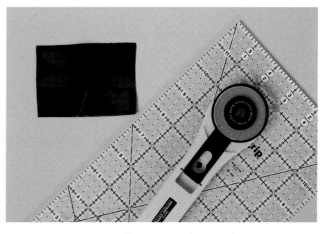

Cut out rectangle.

Free-Motion Embellishment

1. Choose thread for free-motion embellishment. Lay several different threads, such as metallics or rayons, over the fabric to decide which is best.

Blue thread was chosen because it contrasts well with fabric.

2. Thread your machine with the chosen decorative thread. Use invisible thread in the bobbin. Attach a free-motion foot and drop the feed dogs.

3. Carefully outline the one area of the design you wish to feature by free-motion stitching around the lines provided in the print. Then do some fill-in stitching, as was done in the wings.

Free-motion stitch outline with metallic thread, and then fill in the wings.

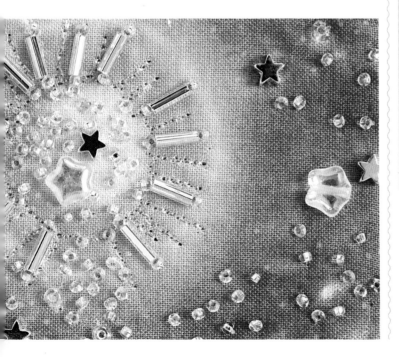

Beading

Now is the best part—we can start to play! The samples have beads applied to the highlighted parts of the design, with a few scattered for added detail. It's really up to you how much detail you want.

1. Apply beads to the surface, using the beading techniques on page 16.

2. When the focal area is beaded, randomly add a bead here and there around the print. It's really not necessary to worry about how neat the back is, because it will be covered later with backing. However, don't let it get too lumpy from knots that will ruin the feel of your card.

Notice that the last few beads on the tail are not done. These will be added after the edge is complete.

Back of stabilizer with beading completed

Backing the ATC

1. Cut the chosen backing fabric to 2½" × 3½". I used a scrap of hand-painted fabric that didn't turn out well enough to use in a quilt but that is just perfect for this technique. Sign or date the backing fabric now, while it is still flat.

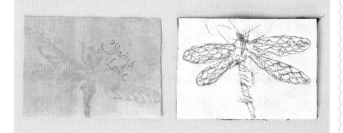

Prepare backing for beaded piece.

2. Spray baste or use a gluestick to adhere the backing fabric to the back of the stabilizer.

Edge Finishing

Use a machine satin stitch (see Finishing the Edges, page 10) to finish the edge of your ATC. You have just finished your ATC and added to your collection!

tassel tip

As you complete your satin stitching, pull the machine threads extra long (about 18˝) before cutting threads away from the machine. With the threads still attached to the project, thread these through a beading needle and string them with beads. First, thread several small beads. Add a larger bead, thread your needle back up through the smaller ones, and anchor the thread in the border stitching. Then do another tassel or two of beads before finally anchoring the thread in the border stitching. This creates dangling tassels on one corner for an extra touch and a different finish.

Beaded print ATCs, 2½" × 3½", with beaded tassels made by Judy Bartel

beaded goddess
Postcards

Turned and stuffed doll with beading

Beaded goddess postcard, 4" × 6", made with simple goddess doll pattern, page 37.

A large part of my stitching and fiber art has been in the field of doll-making. The skills developed in that field are applicable to all of my textile art. I especially like to make dolls—of any size—because they always exude a little bit of attitude or character. This card is one of the most popular I make, as it can be done in color or styles to suit anybody. To allow more space for embellishment and theme, we are going to make a postcard instead of an ATC.

This project will also be a lesson in beginning doll-making. We will make a lightly stuffed doll for an embellishment on a quilted or decorative background. I have also included a more advanced pattern at the end of this project, page 43.

The doll pattern is multipurpose and can be used alone as a pin by simply fastening a brooch pin to the body, vertically, on the back.

Supplies (for each postcard)

* **Fabric for doll, at least 4″ × 8″ square to be folded right sides together**
* **Background fabric for front to accent doll, 4″ × 6″**
* **Backing fabric, 4″ × 6″**
* **Stuffing (I used Soft Touch Polyfil Supreme.)**
* **Heavyweight stabilizer, 4″ × 6″ (I used Timtex.)**
* **Pearl cotton for edging finish**
* **Quilter's Freezer Paper**
* **Seed beads for hair, 1 tube**
* **Various beads for clothing**
* **Thread to match doll fabric**
* **2 Delica beads for eyes *if* you wish to add them (I haven't.)**
* **Chopstick and extra-large drinking straw (or a set of turning tubes)**
* **Gluestick**
* **Free-motion foot**
* **Appliqué foot**

Instructions

Making the Doll

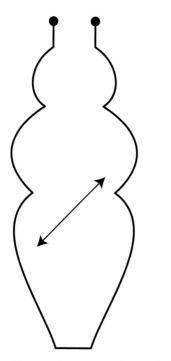

Simple goddess template pattern—Copy at 100%.

1. Trace the doll pattern onto freezer paper but do not cut out the template. Fold the doll fabric in half, right sides together, ensuring the doll pattern fits. Iron the freezer paper template pattern on the bias grain of the folded fabric—that is, *at an angle across the fabric surface.* This puts the actual doll fabric on the bias, allowing it to turn and shape more smoothly.

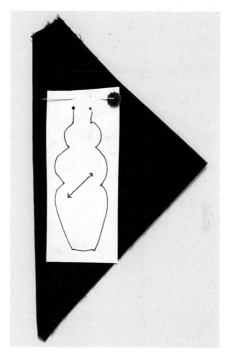

Lay out pattern on bias.

2. Use thread that matches the doll fabric as closely as possible. Set your machine at a very small stitch and sew just outside the line of the template from dot to dot. Reinforce stitching at the dots. The space between the dots is the opening for turning and stuffing.

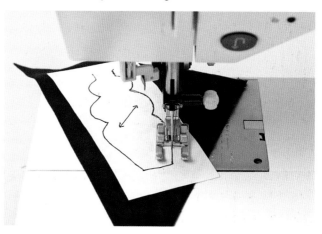

Machine stitch around pattern using open-toe appliqué foot for visibility.

If your fabric has a tendency to fray or if this is your first tiny turned object, it is a good idea to apply fray check all around the seam allowance and across the opening. Let dry before trimming.

3. Remove the paper template. It should just pop off, because the tiny stitches have perforated the paper. Carefully trim this stitched piece to a ⅛" seam allowance. *Refer to the illustration before trimming* and notice the longer "tab" of the seam allowance left at the top of the head. Because the opening often gets worn from the stuffing process, this tab allows for more seam allowance and can simply be turned under into the head for a smooth closure rather than a frayed one. On this project, the closure is at the top of the head because it will be covered with hair and will not be noticed.

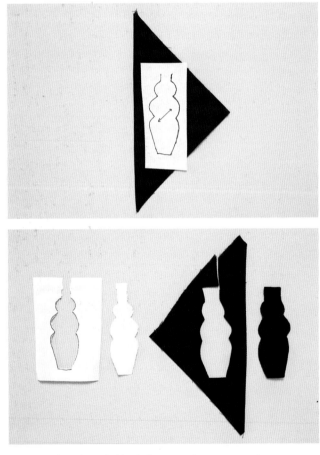

Complete stitching before removing paper template. Trim seams. Note tab at top of head.

4. Turn the doll right side out (see the detailed turning instructions for turning a small item, page 15).

5. When you have turned this little body, use the chopstick through the neck opening to smooth out the shape from the inside. Push the hips and elbow areas out to their max, finger-pressing as you go.

Stuffing the Doll

Do not stuff this little doll too firmly. It is going to be treated more like an appliqué, so it would be inappropriate to have it too thick.

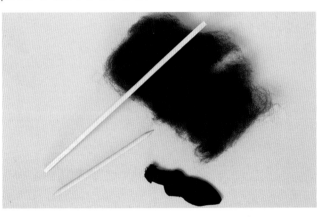

Approximate amount of stuffing to fill small doll

1. The easiest way to stuff a body this small is to use the chopstick. Hold a pinch of stuffing between your fingers against the tip of the chopstick. Twirl the chopstick, winding a small amount onto the tip and forming a sort of swab. Push this tip into the neck opening and all the way down to the feet. Pinch the bump at the feet and pull out the stick. Roll the doll between your fingers to smooth out the stuffing.

Twirl stuffing onto chopstick.

2. Repeat Step 1, allowing a little extra in the tummy and breast areas. When the doll is stuffed to your satisfaction, turn the tab at the top into the head and stitch the seam closed with the same thread used to sew the body. Now she's ready to be embellished.

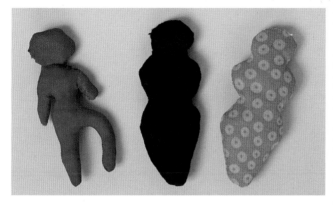

Turned, stuffed, and closed goddesses ready for embellishing

Background

1. Cut a piece of Timtex and a piece of background fabric (that will be an accent to your doll) to 4″ × 6″. I found this project to be an interesting way to use ethnic fabrics. After all, if you're making a postcard, how better to make it look like you've traveled to exotic places?

alternate size tip

Another alternative for this project is to make it an ATC, in which case you would cut your stabilizer to 2½″ × 3½″. Follow the instructions in the same order, simply adjusting the size of the background.

2. Use a gluestick to glue the background fabric to the stabilizer. Enhance the design with free-motion stitching. This also fixes the background fabric and the stabilizer together and makes it easier to embellish.

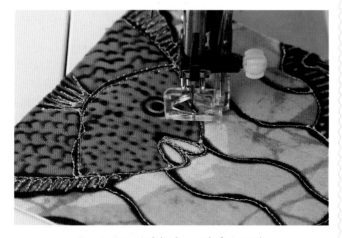

Free-motion stitch background of postcard.

3. Position the doll on the background where she looks best. Plan your embellishments. The beading and embellishing around the body and through the backing will attach the doll to the background. Embellish with items that complement the design theme. In the purple card, I used beads that can be interpreted as baskets or drums; the fishing tackle enhances the theme in the orange card.

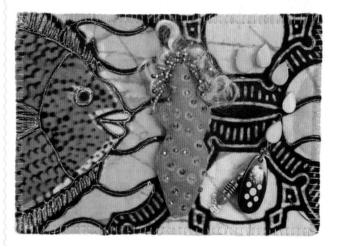

Embellishments enhance the postcard's theme.

Beading the Hair and Body

1. Bring the needle up from the back, through the background fabric, and through the edge of the head. As shown, take the thread through a number of beads (the hair strands on the samples use from 4 to 6 beads). Lay the thread of beads over your finger and run the needle back through all *except* the last bead and then down through the background. Make some bead strands fall along the edge of the head and some behind the head stitched only through the background. To make the hair strand stand out from the fabric, pull tight and backstitch. Use a variety of tight strands and loose, dangling strands to get the look of hair, as shown in the finished postcards.

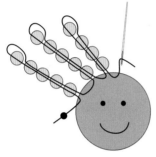

Beaded hair stitch

thread tip

When making the hair, it is a very good idea to rub the thread you are using across some beeswax or Thread Heaven thread conditioner to keep it from twisting. This will save you much frustration.

securing beads tip

Add a double backstitch every second or third pass in case of thread breakage.

2. The rest of the beadwork around the doll is basically a stab stitch. Attach the doll body to the background with threaded beads. Simply come up through the backing, filling the thread with the number of beads to wrap the leg or tummy, and come back down through the backing again.

Stab stitch with threaded beads to attach body to background.

3. Continue beading and stitching until you feel your card is appropriately embellished.

Backing the Postcard

The backing fabric for the postcard should be plain enough to write or print a message on, but it should still have sufficient color to prevent any embellishing threads from showing through. Before attaching the backing, I do some stitching to make it look like a postcard.

To make space for the message, I stitch a vertical line down the middle and add three straight horizontal lines for the address. It is fun to find a piece of fabric suitable for fussy cutting a postage stamp shape. Simply cut the shape with pinking shears and sew it down with a straight stitch and raw edge. Add your personal note and address with a permanent marking pen.

Finished backs of postcards

Edging done with a machine buttonhole stitch, using
Sulky Holoshimmer thread in top and bobbin

Edging done by hand with heavy thread designed for bobbin work

Edge Finishing

It is perfectly acceptable to finish the edge on this project with the machine satin stitch. For the sake of variety, however, let's try a buttonhole stitch. This stitch can be done by machine, by hand, **or** by hand with beads added. Your choice of thread should be governed by its strength and ability to pierce and pass through the postcard layers without fraying. (See Finishing the Edges, page 10.)

Postcards, 4″ × 6″, made by Judy Bartel—notice the hand buttonhole edging with beads.

bonus project: Pin Dolls

This advanced doll pattern or the simpler doll pattern can be used to make a tiny pin doll or brooch that can be worn on your lapel, your sun hat, your handbag, or whatever you wish to embellish with a little doll.

Two finished ATCs using advanced doll pattern

The doll attached to the ATCs shown here is made from the more advanced pattern, with arms, legs, and a separate head. It is done in exactly the same way as the simpler doll, but the turning and stuffing are a bit trickier. It is well worth mastering this little lady, as the skills involved—patience, gentleness, and caution—will enable you to turn fingers on more advanced dolls or any other shape you may wish to add to your textile art.

Instructions

Here are some finer points of turning and stuffing to remember for this more advanced doll shape.

1. Trace the pattern on freezer paper and place it on the bias of the folded fabric, rights sides together.

2. Stitch. When doing the tiny stitching around the shape, make 2 tiny stitches across the underarms and between the legs. This allows a space (albeit teensy) to clip into and makes it easier to turn (see Turned Pieces with Small Openings, page 15).

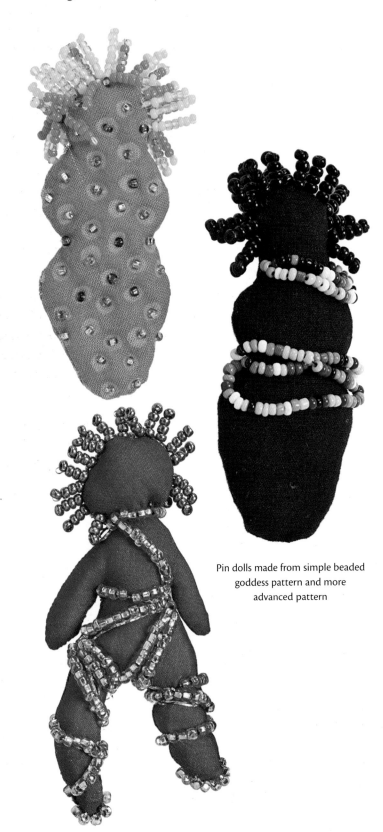

Pin dolls made from simple beaded goddess pattern and more advanced pattern

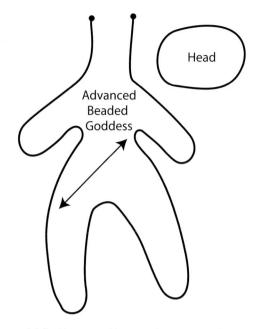

Head

Advanced
Beaded
Goddess

Advanced doll with arms and legs template pattern—Copy at 100%.

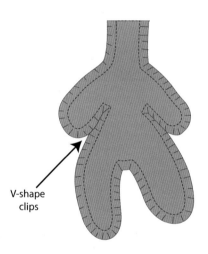

V-shape
clips

Stitch and clipping detail for doll with
arms and legs

3. When turning this small body with legs and arms, start with one leg. Put the straw or turning tube down that leg and insert the stick at the seam allowance, sliding the leg down onto the stick. Only push the leg up until the foot can be seen through the neck. Repeat this step with the other leg and with both arms. The neck opening will seem quite full, but it is best to get all the tips turned before turning the body.

4. Pinch the body between your thumb and fingers of one hand. With your other hand, pinch the doll's toe and finger-tips. Gently pull the tips while rolling the body between your thumb and fingers. The tips will emerge easily; do not pull too hard, as this can pop your stitching. A smooth set

of tweezers or a hemostat can help with this step. Again, the greatest skill in this tiny turning is to go slowly and patiently.

5. Stuffing is done with the same method of making little swabs and pushing one into each leg and then each arm. When the legs and arms are filled, add some stuffing to the center body. Turn in the neck edges and do a few quick stitches to hold it closed. When attaching to the card, attach the body first in the position you prefer; then place the head over the neck tip.

6. To make the head, iron the freezer paper pattern on top of two layers of fabric. Sew the oval shape for the head, right sides together, in a complete circle. To turn it, snip a small opening in the back and turn with the same tube-stick method as before. Stuff the head through this hole in the back. You can stitch this little hole closed and cover it with beading. Or you can attach the head flat against any size card. If you stitch the head down, nobody will ever know there's a hole anywhere. For a brooch, the head is stitched chin to neck to add it to the body.

7. To make the bead hair for a pin doll, rather than just doing it around the crown of the head, apply little strands all over the back too. Embellish or dress the doll in whatever way you wish. When embellishment is complete, attach a pin (available at the local craft store) to the back. You have a new brooch. These make great little gifts.

painted hibiscus
Postcard

Painting fabric, free-motion stitching, beading, and satin stitching

Painted Hibiscus postcard, 4″ × 6″

I am not an expert on the subject of painting fabric, but I can tell you that painting fabric is rewarding and adds to your project's originality. The most important thing about painting fabric is to approach it with a carefree attitude. Try **not** to plan what you want to achieve. Just paint in the colors and work with what you get. Often the serendipitous results are better than what you would have planned.

A good reference for more information on painting fabric is the wonderfully extensive and detailed book **Skydyes** by painter Mickey Lawler, available from C&T Publishing. The following are some points that I can tell you from my own experience:

* Painting fabric outside in summer, rather than inside in the winter, is easier and produces better results.

* Choose a fine-weave white cotton and cut it into workable sizes. The whiter the cotton, the brighter your colors.

* Prewash your fabric and press lightly before painting. That makes it prepared for dyeing (PFD).

* I use Setacolor and Lumiere paints. Both can be diluted with water, which also lightens the resulting color.

* Good equipment to have on hand includes brushes, sea sponges, rubber stamps, spray bottles, plastic water containers, plastic plates for mixing paints, and a plastic sheet to protect your work surface.

* The fabric will pick up any texture on your painting surface, which can be an advantage or a disadvantage. I use a foam

core board from the local stationery shop and cover it with adhesive plastic contact paper for my painting surface.

* Pin your fabric to the foam core board so that it doesn't move when you are painting.

* Spritz the fabric with a light mist of water. If the fabric is too wet, the colors will bleed; if too dry, they won't spread well. Try a test piece first.

* The colors dry lighter than they look when wet. Use a test scrap; sometimes this lightness turns out to be something spectacular.

* I paint several coats, drying in between, and then stamp on it. Although this is not a great idea for quilts that will be washed, it is not an issue with these projects.

* Keep track of the steps so that when you get one you really like, you can try it again. Take a picture, too.

* It's much like faux finishing a wall in your house—if you've ever done that. Different applications produce different results:

> Try a sea sponge to add multiple colors.

> Use a paintbrush to apply paint.

> Scrunch up your fabric after painting to create darker ridges as it dries.

> Sprinkle with salt while still wet, let dry, and brush off.

> Use a dye inkpad to stamp designs on the painted cloth when it has dried.

* Apply fabric paint onto the stamp with a dry brush and stamp on your painted cloth. Don't repaint your stamp every time. Sometimes a partial impression adds to the design elements.

* Heat set the painted fabric with a dry iron.

Moist fabric brush-painted with a light green background with darker green maple leaves stamped on surface after first dried coat

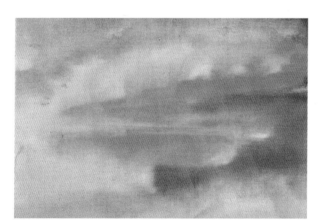

Fabric sprayed lightly with water, then brushed with streaks of golden yellow, followed quickly by orange, red, and purple

Sample of multicolor sponged fabric, dried and finished with metallic paint applied with maple leaf rubber stamp

Piece streaked with rose color mixed with a little yellow. A few more streaks of yellow were added and the fabric spritzed again. When dry, the backs of real leaves were lightly brushed with fabric paint and pressed onto the fabric.

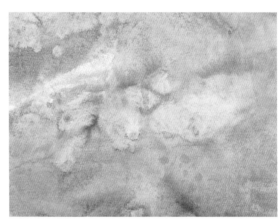

Very damp fabric scrunched into a loose ball with a blue-violet mixture dabbed on top. The top ridges were then touched up with a bit of pearl metallic paint.

Using a sea sponge, moist fabric was dabbed with grays, brown, and rusty red. It was then spritzed, dried, and then sponged again with metallic copper.

Supplies

- **Tightly woven white cotton, ¼ yard**
- **Heavyweight stabilizer, 4″ × 6″ (I used Timtex.)**
- **Backing fabric, 4″ × 6″**
- **Paintbrushes (from ½″ to 1″ wide), flat with real hair**
- **Pebeo Setacolor Transparent watercolor fabric paints (Light Green 27, Moss Green 28, Titanium White 10, Blue Cobalt 11, Vermillion Red 26)**
- **Jacquard acrylic (Ruby Red 107)**
- **Lumiere acrylic (True Gold 550)**
- **Painting surface**
- **Container for mixing paints**
- **Pins**
- **Iron**
- **Green, yellow, and red thread**
- **Yellow seed beads**
- **Squirt bottle for misting fabric**
- **Free-motion foot**

Instructions

This quick and easy project will introduce you to playing with paints on fabric. You will notice that this process gets better and better as you go along and that the stitching, beading, and edge finishing are surprisingly easy and pretty. Clean brushes after painting with each color.

1. Cut a piece of cotton fabric about 6″ × 8″ each and pin the dry fabric to the painting surface.

2. For the light green and the light red, mix a dab of Setacolor Transparent paint with an equal amount of water in a yogurt lid or something similar. Mix with the large paintbrush.

3. Using the light green paint on the smaller brush, outline and fill in the 2 leaves.

Add petals and outline leaves.

6. After the piece is dry, mix the darker red paint by Jacquard with an equal amount of water. Use the smaller brush to add veins to the flower petals. Set aside to dry.

Paint 2 leaves.

4. Use the smaller brush and the light red paint to add a vague representation of petals.

5. Mix some dark green paint with an equal amount of water and use it to outline the leaves. Add lines to represent the veins. Set aside to dry.

Add darker lines to red flower.

7. After the piece is dry, use the larger brush to mix the blue and white together with water to get a nice sky blue. Apply the sky blue paint to the dried fabric between the leaves and petals. Quickly squirt the fabric with water to wet the entire surface. This will cause the blue to bleed into all the wet areas that don't already have paint on them, giving the background a textured look rather than a solid blue. Set aside to dry.

Add the sky blue background.

8. Use the larger brush to apply gold metallic paint mixed with water to *the petals and the leaves only*. Set aside to dry.

Apply metallic gold to painted hibiscus.

9. Press with a dry iron to heat set the colors. Trim the piece to 4″ × 6″.

10. Layer the painted hibiscus piece with the stabilizer and secure the layers using a gluestick. Attach the free-motion foot to your sewing machine and outline the leaves and veins with green thread.

11. Change to red thread and stitch lines in the petals.

12. Change to yellow thread and stitch a circle of yellow in the center of the hibiscus.

Free-motion stitching lines on painted hibiscus

13. Use yellow thread to stitch a cluster of yellow beads on top of the yellow circle.

14. Use a gluestick to secure the backing fabric to the underside of the postcard.

15. Finish the edge as you like. The pictured sample was done with an ordinary machine satin stitch and yellow thread in both the bobbin and the needle.

16. Don't forget to sign your artwork!

fused landscape
Postcards

Curved cutting, fusing, satin stitching, elementary beading, and embellishment

Fused landscape postcards, 4″ × 6″, with satin stitching and simple embellishments

These cards were inspired by the designs of a Canadian artist named Ted Harrison. His painting style uses very strong, bright colors. A strong line of black often separates each area of color. In this project, the satin stitching represents this line.

This project is designed to give you an easy way to try a landscape. When you finish, you will have four completed postcards, each one individual in design.

Supplies

* **Scraps of fabric in landscape colors and prints, each a minimum of 2″ × 9″**
* **Backing fabric, 1 fat quarter**
* **Heavyweight stabilizer, 9″ × 12″ (I used Timtex.)**
* **Double-sided fusible webbing, 1 yard (I used Steam-A-Seam 2.)**
* **Threads for landscape**
* **Lingerie thread or invisible thread for bobbin**
* **Embellishments, such as buttons, beads, and so on**
* **Rotary cutter and acrylic ruler**
* **2 pressing cloths**

L andscapes appeal to everyone. Each person may have a preference for mountain, ocean, forest, or even city landscapes, but it's easy to assume that everybody can appreciate the beauty of nature in some respect. Because nature has an incredible sense of artistry, it is difficult to make a fabric interpretation of a landscape that can be considered "wrong."

Instructions

Preparing Fabric Strips

fusible webbing tip

It is possible to do this strip piecing and cutting with fabric that hasn't been treated with fusible webbing. You could use a spray adhesive to attach it to the backing before satin stitching. However, you will find that the untreated fabric has little threads that poke through the satin stitching, whereas the fabric attached with fusible webbing gives you a cleaner edge.

1. Cover your pressing surface with a pressing cloth. Place your fusible web on the pressing cloth and remove the top layer of release paper.

2. Lay the 2″ × 9″ strips of fabric in rows across the fusible web. Small overlaps will not matter, as they will be discarded when you do the curved cutting.

3. Cover with another pressing cloth. Press until all fabrics are firmly attached to the adhesive on the fusible web. Do not remove the second paper backing yet.

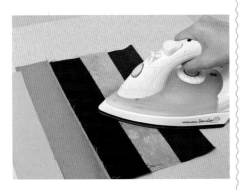

Press strips of color to Steam-A-Seam 2.

Cutting Strips into Shapes

Move the piece of fused fabric to your cutting mat and use a rotary cutter to cut gently curved lines through each color strip to represent the contours of hills, valleys, sky, or the straight lines of a lake.

Laying Out Landscape Colors

1. It is a good idea to start with a fabric representing sky in the center of the stabilizer. I used a strip of yellow that was not one of the curved, fused fabric pieces. I used a gluestick to secure this fabric strip to the stabilizer.

Initial layout for sky portion of landscape

2. Add your tree or mountain fabric curved strips. This can be several strips or just one, depending on what you are trying to represent. Remove the paper backing from the fused strips as you place them in your design.

Beginning hills and features of landscape

3. Add a piece for water and overlap it with another curved piece representing a hill of forest colors.

4. Add fabric that represents the ground at both the top and bottom edges.

5. Cover with a pressing cloth and press these strips to the heavyweight stabilizer.

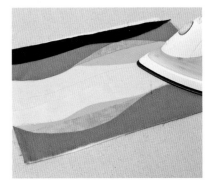

Press curved strips to stabilizer.

Satin Stitching Landscape Lines

1. Choose a top thread color for the satin stitching. The bobbin thread can be lingerie or invisible thread, as it will not be seen once the card is finished.

satin stitch tip

Try out various widths of satin stitch on a scrap of stabilizer with fabric fused to it. This will help you determine the stitch setting to use on your cards.

2. Apply a tight satin stitch over every line where one fabric meets another. You can do every line the same color or vary the colors to match the fabrics they are covering.

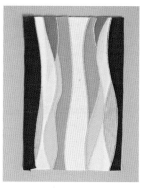

Satin stitch curved strips to stabilizer.

Backing, Cutting, and Finishing

1. Use a ruler and rotary cutter to trim overhanging fabrics from all 4 sides. This will make for a neater card when you are finished.

2. Satin stitch a sun motif and any other *stitching* embellishments before adding the backing.

3. Place the trimmed piece on a 9″ × 12″ piece of backing fabric that has been sprayed with adhesive or has fusible webbing on its back side. Smooth in place with your fingers to stick the layers together firmly.

4. Use a pressing cloth and press with a dry iron. Be sure there are no wrinkles and that all the raw edges will be covered with stitching.

5. Use a cutting mat, a clear plastic ruler, and a rotary cutter to trim all the outside edges evenly. Then cut the piece in half horizontally through the skyline. Turn the ruler and cut the piece vertically in half. You now have four cards, each approximately 4½″ × 6″.

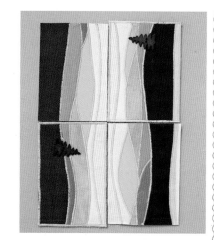

Four postcards from one background

6. This embellishing step is optional: You can add star sequins in the sky, flower sequins along the earth, fish beads in the water, a bright yellow button in the sky to represent a sun, or even a little tree on a hillside.

7. Machine satin stitch (see Finishing the Edges, page 10) the outer edges. Use the same thread as was used for the landscape satin stitching.

Satin-stitched edges

And there you have it—four completed cards in one basic project. Isn't it interesting how different each one looks?

bonus project: Landscape Wallhanging

Serene Landscape, 11″ × 13″ by Judy Bartel

Instructions

This wallhanging is made exactly the same way as the Fused Landscape Postcards, except without the satin stitching and it isn't cut into four pieces.

1. Cut fused, curved strips and fuse them to the Timtex in a pleasing arrangement, starting with the sky color at the top instead of the center.

2. Stitch the strips into place with an invisible thread.

3. Enhance the landscape effect with some straight stitching and embellishments.

4. Straight stitch the landscape onto another background with a folded top for hanging (see *Red Dragonfly Wallhanging*, page 57, for instructions on this backing style).

ginkgo leaves
Wallhanging

Textured background, double fusing, top stitching, curved seams, twin-needle top stitching, fused and top-stitched leaves, turned leaves with couched threads, and beading

Ginkgo Leaves Wallhanging, 14¾" × 19¼"

With this project, we will explore fusing, texture, and top stitching. Sometimes a plain pieced and quilted background just isn't a spectacular enough backdrop for the feature item. When this is the case, my favorite way to make it come to life is to texture the background with top stitching.

Supplies

* 3 coordinating background fabrics, ⅝ yard each (see Fabric Tip, page 53)

* Dupioni silks, lamés, or other decorative fabrics in various colors, 6 fat quarters (minimum)

* Fabric for backing, 1 fat quarter

* Batting, 18″ × 22″

* Double-sided fusible webbing, ½ yard

* Quilter's Freezer Paper for leaf templates

* Thread to coordinate with background fabrics

* Twin needle (I did my sample with Schmetz 130/705, 60/100.)

* Top-stitching threads (1 or 2 colors)

* Lingerie thread for bobbin

* Decorative yarn or thread for couching the turned leaf, 5 yards

* Multiple colors of decorative threads for top and bobbin on fused leaves

* 3 dyed silk rods, driftwood, or twigs to represent branches

* Pressing cloth

* Beads

* Rotary cutter, mat, and acrylic ruler

Multiple colors of decorative threads were used in topstitching the ginkgo leaves. I like to use metallic threads for sparkle and color, as well as threads that provide color and sheen.

In this sample, I used Ackerman Viscose, Brother Gold Metallic, Isafil Viscose, Madeira Metallic, Mettler Metallic, Mettler Polysheen, Oliver Twist space-dyed sewing cotton, Robison Anton Rayon, Sulky Ultra Twist, and Wonderfil Mirage.

In choosing fabrics for the background, you must decide whether the pieces will look best cut with the design going the length of the fabric or from selvage to selvage. This can alter the amount required.

Fabrics used in background have different print directions.

Instructions

Cutting and Sewing Background

First we will make the background. I do not prewash fabrics that are going to be part of wall art, as I feel the sizing keeps them fresher for a longer period of time. However, if you are using fabric that you have already washed, this will not present a problem.

1. Cut the yardage in half across the printed design to make pieces approximately 18″ × 22″ long, with the print oriented lengthwise on the pieces.

2. Refer to Cutting and Piecing Curved Seams, page 12, for instructions on this piecing technique. Piece the fabric, creating curved seams, until the width of the background is about 20″ wide. This background is meant to represent tree bark, so it should have lots of random curves. Keep in mind that the next part of the process will take up some of that width.

Twin-Needle Top Stitching for Texture

Topstitch the pieced fabric to add texture. Refer to Twin-Needle Top Stitching, page 13, for details on this technique.

I used an Oliver Twist hand-dyed thread and a Wonderfil Mirage cotton thread. With this combination, sometimes the eye sees the shimmer of the rayon thread, and sometimes it sees the cotton, adding to its natural look.

This texturing puckers occasionally, but keep in mind that bark isn't perfect, so your ridges don't have to be either! When putting together the background panel, keep in mind that the width of the background panel will shrink by up to 4″, depending on the width of the twin needle and the amount of top stitching done. Press the top-stitched background with a steam iron.

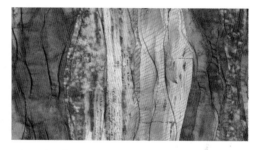

Completed twin-needle top stitching of background

Making the Ginkgo Leaves

For the leaves, gather silks, lamés, and other specialty fabrics in the colorway of your choice. Lay them out over the background to audition them. I have used sand-washed silk, cotton lamé, and dupioni silk. It is good to have a mixture of shimmering fabrics as well as some that are less so. These leaves can also be made of cotton, but I prefer the sparkle.

Audition leaf fabrics on background.

1. Prefuse the leaf fabric following the directions for Double-Fused Fabrics, page 14. Use a different color fabric on each side. Making the leaves a different color on each side allows for flipping them over in the layout stage for extra color choices.

2. Use a copy machine to enlarge the templates, page 55, to 200%. Trace the templates onto freezer paper. I prefer cutting out the leaf templates with paper scissors *before* pressing them to the fabric, because I hate to use my best scissors on paper. Doing this also allows me to lay out the templates on my specialty fabrics, producing the least waste. Each template indicates the number of leaves needed for this project, so you can estimate how much fabric you will need to fuse.

3. Press these patterns onto your previously fused fabrics and cut out with fabric scissors.

leaf tip

I like to make extra leaves so I can play with the layout and colors to get what I want. When laying out your leaf templates, leave some extra stem room and extend the stem when you cut it out. It is always nice to have extra stem to twist or curl, and it's easier to snip off what is in the way rather than wish it were ¼″ longer.

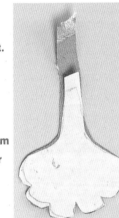

Add extra length to stem of pattern.

4. Pin the background to a design wall or lay it out on the cutting table. Decide which color leaves to use where. This layout process (before stitching on the leaves) will help you decide where the colors will look best on your project. When the leaves are topstitched, they will curl in a very natural way. However, they curl *upward*, so it is wise to decide which side of a two-color leaf is facing out before proceeding. When you find a layout design you particularly like, take a picture of it for later reference.

Play with cut leaf arrangements on background *before* stitching leaves. This allows for variations with threadwork to add highlights where needed.

Decorative Top Stitching Fused Leaves

This really is just a simple straight stitch going back and forth over the leaf to imitate vein lines. Refer to the photo of the finished leaves.

1. Choose the top and bobbin threads. They will be part of the design, so choose them carefully. Set up your machine with a fine needle (size 75/11) and a regular stitch length (2.5).

2. Stitch from the top of the stem down to the leaf's outside edge. Stitch right off the edge, backstitch, and stop with the needle down in the leaf. (Stitching over the edge holds the leaf together if the fusing gives out.) Lift the foot and turn the leaf. Stitch back up on the same line.

Stitched lines make the leaves curl upward.

The Turned Leaf

The top leaf on this wallhanging is a turned leaf. Choose two colors of silk, but do **not** fuse them together. Use the largest ginkgo leaf pattern, below. See Turned Pieces with Small Openings, page 15, for directions to make this leaf.

Couching the Leaves

See Couching with Decorative Threads, page 14, for directions on adding decorative yarn to the leaves. In choosing thread colors, I use natural colors, because I want the threads to be as discreet as possible so that the feature is the couched strand of yarn. The bobbin thread should match the bottom side of the leaf as closely as possible, because it will show on the back. If the final arrangement has a leaf lifted from the surface, a thread that contrasts would be distracting.

Attaching the Leaf Elements

1. Pin the turned leaf at the top and the fused leaves cascading below it. The fused leaves will be stitched onto the background by hand, with beads added randomly to represent dewdrops. The elements that cascade over the finished edge of the wallhanging will be added after the backing is added and edges are finished.

2. Add silk rods to represent branches for the leaf stems to curl around. You can use driftwood or twigs to duplicate this look; however, the silk rods are easy to sew *through* with beads.

Turned and couched leaf attached to background with scattered beads. Note use of silk rods representing branches. Stem wrapped around silk rod with additional beads. Note curl in leaves.

Applying Backing and Batting

1. Trim the embellished background to size. Careful measuring ensures an even rectangle. I trimmed mine to 15¼" × 19¾", allowing a ¼" seam allowance for turning. Your piece may vary in size—this is art and not an exact reproduction.

2. To finish this project, follow the directions for Pillowcase Finish, page 11.

Quilting

Quilting this project is very simple and is only done to hold the layers together.

1. Start with a line of decorative thread ¼" in from the edge all around the rectangle. Using a walking foot can be helpful.

2. Stitch from the top to the bottom along several of the twin-needle stitched lines, using the same color thread as was used in the topstitching. Sew a tiny backstitch at the stop and start to secure the quilting lines. The area with the leaves cannot be quilted all the way, so start at the top and go down to where it ends behind a leaf. Turn the piece and do the same from the bottom up.

3. Once the quilting is done, add some final embellishments. I added a cluster of beads here and there, carefully stitching through to the back in exactly the same place so that it stayed neat. At this point, I was struck by a bit of whimsy and added one more leaf cascading off the edge to make it look more natural.

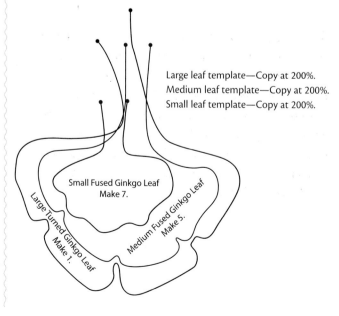

Large leaf template—Copy at 200%.
Medium leaf template—Copy at 200%.
Small leaf template—Copy at 200%.

Small Fused Ginkgo Leaf
Make 7.

Large Turned Ginkgo Leaf
Make 1.

Medium Fused Ginkgo Leaf
Make 5.

bonus project: Ginkgo Leaf ATC Pocket Page

An ATC pocket page is a great storage idea. And working on a little larger scale than an ATC can be appealing.

Ginkgo Leaf ATC pocket page, 5″ × 6″ finished

Supplies

* **Surface fabric (dupioni silk, taffeta, lace, or whatever strikes your fancy), 5½″ × 6½″**

* **Heavyweight stabilizer, 5½″ × 6½″ (I used Timtex.)**

* **Backing fabric, 5½″ × 6½″ (a good place to use heavily painted fabric)**

* **5 completed fused medium fabric leaves of your color choice (See page 54 and use templates on page 55)**

* **1 large turned ginkgo leaf (See page 55 and use templates on page 55)**

* **Variety of decorative threads and yarns for couching the turned leaf**

* **Beads to embellish the 5 fused leaves and parts of the background**

* **Gluestick or double-sided webbing**

Instructions

1. Apply the surface fabric to the Timtex with a gluestick or double-sided fusible webbing.

2. Lay out 5 fused fabric leaves in a pleasing arrangement in the top left corner, keeping well within ½″ of the edge to allow room for finishing. Let one leaf disappear over the edges.

3. Hand stitch up through the back of the Timtex and through the small leaves, occasionally catching a bead on your needle before going through to the back. Curl the stem and add as many beads as you want.

4. Place the turned and couched leaf on the bottom right corner so it covers a good part of the page, but allow the edges to overlap the right side and along the bottom side. Pin in place.

5. Place the backing fabric face down on top of the embellished surface.

6. Starting on the bottom seam approximately 1″ from the bottom left corner, sew a couple backstitches. Then stitch the 3 layers together with a ¼″ seam. Stop ¼″ from the corner with the needle down and pivot to sew the side seam. Make sure you catch the turned leaf in the side and bottom seams and the fused leaf in the top and side seams. Do *not* catch the fused leaves that you want left free. Continue stitching until you are on the bottom seam again. Stop to leave a 2″ opening for turning the project. Backstitch where you end the stitching.

7. Trim the seam allowance to ⅛″ and clip the 4 corners.

8. Turn the page through the opening. Note how the turned leaf has now formed a pocket.

9. Hand stitch the open seamline closed.

10. Gently press the edges of the page to flatten and straighten.

11. Choose a decorative top stitch on your machine and stitch a line ¼″ all the way around the page. Further embellish the page by adding beads to the seamline.

You can fasten this page to similar pages in a variety of ways. Using a firm stabilizer will allow several pages to be joined in booklike fashion to stand on display. A pocket can be added to the opposite side of the page as well so that each side holds an ATC. These pages provide an appealing way to display your ATC collection and to garner admiration of your textile art.

red dragonfly Wallhanging

Painting fabric, painting batting, stamping fabric, fusing and stamping organza, thread painting fused organza, raw-edge backing with a ready-made hanging tube

Red Dragonfly Wallhanging, 13″ × 19″

first tried this technique on a large fractured landscape wall quilt that I was making for our home. I had a piece of fabric that was perfect for one area, but it was too plain to fit in well with the rest of the fabrics used. On a whim, I decided to try stamping a design on it. The results were perfect, adding just the right amount of detail in an area that needed more.

Stamping a design on fabric also gives a nice drawing outline if you are not comfortable drawing an object on your own. Since my successful experiment, I have enhanced a lot of my work with rubber stamps and decorative thread. A beautiful quilt done by my soul mate, Judy Bartel, inspired this particular project.

Why a red dragonfly? In early November, I was at a quilting retreat with my favorite art quilting friends. It was a beautiful day, with the sun shining and no rain. Because it was so beautiful outside, we decided to take advantage of the moment and eat our lunch outside. We were all laughing and enjoying ourselves when a red dragonfly flitted across our table, catching everyone's attention. He flew up in the air behind us and landed on my back! I was told to put my head down so the people on the other side of the table could admire him, too. But I couldn't see him. So I've created my own red dragonfly here and hid a second dragonfly near the water. I hope you enjoy them both.

Sunset on San Pedro, 32" × 37½" inspiration quilt by Judy Bartel

Please remember that you can interpret these instructions to suit any stamp that you may have in your possession. I have included ideas for other stamps. The source for this particular stamp is included in the Resources, page 95.

Variety of stamps

Supplies

* **White pima cotton (very fine weave), 12" × 19"**
* **Bleached white cotton quilt batting, 13" × 20"**
* **Backing fabric, 14" × 24"**
* **6 organza strips, in 3 shades for grass, 4" × 20" (I used taupe and 2 shades of green.)**
* **6 double-sided fusible web strips, 3½" × 19"**
* **4 organza squares in colors to match dragonflies, 4" × 4" (I used red and blue.)**
* **2 lightweight fusible web (Steam-A-Seam Lite) squares, 4" × 4"***
* **2 Tear-Away stabilizer squares, 4" × 4"***
* **Dragonfly rubber stamp and others**
* **Fabric paint (Pebeo or Jacquard)—chocolate brown, lime green, vermillion red, royal blue, forest green, black, gold metallic, and blue metallic**
* **Decorative beads**
* **Disposable foam or soft fine bristle brush, 2" wide**
* **Sponge for painting**
* **Decorative threads to complement your stamped design**
* **Threads for decorative stitching on grass and dragonfly**
* **Invisible thread**
* **Matching sewing thread for securing 3-D grass and dragonflies**
* **Quilter's Freezer Paper**
* **Branch or small dowel, approximately 21" long**
* **Foam core for working surface**
* **Spray bottle for water**
* **2 pressing cloths**
* **Spray adhesive**
* **Walking foot**
* **Free-motion foot**
* *** Size squares to cover stamped areas**

Instructions

Fabric Painting

1. Pin dry fabric to the foam core work surface so it stays stretched out.

2. Use a damp sponge to dab the fabric sparingly with chocolate brown paint that has been mixed with an equal part of water.

3. Wash the sponge, squeeze well, and use it to dab the same fabric sparingly with forest green paint mixed with water. Repeat with vermillion red paint. Let dry completely.

4. Spritz the fabric with water until it is quite damp.

5. Use a 2″-wide brush to paint all over the top area with lime green. Do the same to paint the bottom area with royal blue. Spritz the area where the 2 colors meet, so they blend naturally. Let dry.

6. Mix some forest green paint with a tiny bit of black and an equal amount of water. Paint this over the lime green area, purposely missing some spots. Let dry.

7. Mix gold metallic paint with an equal amount of water and brush liberally over the painted top area.

8. Mix blue metallic paint with an equal amount of water and brush over the blue area. Don't hesitate to let some gold go into the water area and some blue go into the green area. Let dry completely.

9. Heat set with a hot, dry iron.

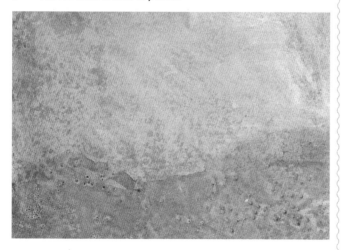

Painted background

Batting Painting

Because this panel is finished with raw edges, I cut the batting panel a little larger and painted it for added effect.

1. Wet the batting thoroughly and squeeze dry.

2. Pin the batting on foam core board (be sure not to tug and separate it).

3. Put a measure of paint in a yogurt or other container and add an equal amount of water. (I used the cap from a beverage bottle to measure).

4. Stir well with a wide foam brush. Use the brush to dab paint onto the edges of the batting, squashing it in so it goes through to the other side. Saturate the batting edges with paint.

5. Squirt the batting square with water so it is saturated. This will blend and spread the paint. Don't paint the center, as it won't show.

6. *Keep flat to dry* so the colors don't run toward the downhill edge and turn muddy. Because the batting is very saturated, it will take overnight to dry if you are working in the winter. If you are lucky enough to be painting in the summer (highly recommended), it will dry quickly outside but should still be kept flat.

Samples of painted batting

Fabric Stamping

Stamping fabric makes it your own unique piece. It also allows those of us who feel insecure with our drawing skills to produce a satisfying design.

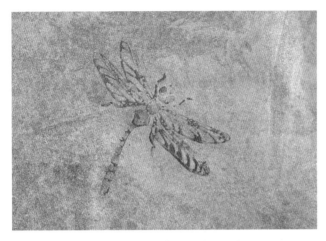

Stamped dragonfly on background

Try your stamping technique on other fabrics first. The sample piece may turn out to be special enough to use for other projects.

1. Press the painted fabric smooth. This gives the best surface possible for the rubber stamp. Lay the pressed fabric flat on your work surface.

2. Use a dry foam brush and vermillion red and royal blue paint straight out of the bottle for each dragonfly. Apply paint sparingly to the rubber stamp. (I stamped 2 dragonflies on my design area, using a different paint color at a time, of course!) Be careful not to get excess amounts in the stamp crevices; excess paint will make a blot in the design.

3. Firmly press the stamp onto the fabric and hold in place for a few seconds.

4. Lift the stamp straight up off the fabric to prevent smudging. Apply as many stamped designs as you wish. Set aside to dry.

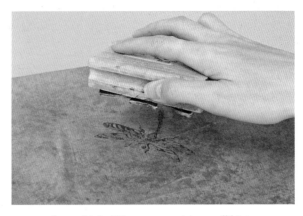

Stamp fabric, lifting stamp straight up off fabric.

5. Heat set with a dry iron.

Thread Painting

Once it is dried and heat set, this piece is ready to be "painted" with decorative threads. In the stamped areas, you will need a stabilizer behind the fabric so that it doesn't bunch up while you work.

1. Working with one area at a time, place the stamped, dried, heat-set background on top of a square of tear-away stabilizer so the stamped design is over the stabilizer. (The stabilizer should be large enough to cover the stamped area.) Pin this area to secure it. The pins can be removed after the first outline stitches are complete.

2. With a free-motion foot and the feed dogs down, thread your machine with a decorative thread that accentuates the design. The bobbin thread should match the top thread.

3. Do 1 stitch, putting the needle down through the fabric so that it brings the tail of the bobbin thread up to the surface. Hold both threads between your thumb and forefinger and make the first 3 or 4 stitches in the same spot to anchor the threads.

4. Outline and fill in the stamped design. It isn't necessary to cover every portion of the design; leave some paint showing through to accent the design. I used Sulky Holoshimmer to outline the dragonfly and a lighter color of the same type of thread for the lines within the wings.

5. After you have applied each color, anchor the threads by stitching in the same place for 3 or 4 stitches.

6. When the design is complete, carefully tear edges of the stabilizer away from the back of the stitching. Repeat Steps 1–5 for the second dragonfly.

Stamped and stitched designs on the background, showing thread painting on front and stabilizer on back

Adding 3-D Embellishments

To enhance the piece and give the dragonflies a place to rest, I added long stalks of grass. I used the double-fused method, except that for these grass blades, I used a **double** layer of fusible web to give the organza more body. Although a firmer fabric would not require this double layer, I chose organza for its shimmer. Preheat your iron to a **low** heat setting for the organza, as it will melt if the iron is too hot. Practice on some organza scraps to find the best heat setting. Fuse the strips of organza in pairs for cutting the blades of grass (see Double-Fused Fabrics, page 14). When you finish, you'll have three fused panels of organza in colors of your choice.

1. Use a copy machine to enlarge the templates to 200%. Trace the grass templates, below, onto freezer paper and cut out on the lines. Each template indicates how many of each piece to make.

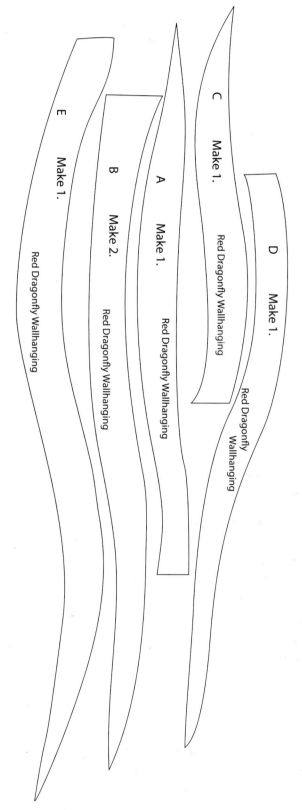

E Make 1. — Red Dragonfly Wallhanging

B Make 2. — Red Dragonfly Wallhanging

A Make 1. — Red Dragonfly Wallhanging

C Make 1. — Red Dragonfly Wallhanging

D Make 1. — Red Dragonfly Wallhanging

Grass template patterns A–E—Copy at 200%.

2. Press the templates onto each of the fused layer sets and stitch a straight-stitch outline around each pattern in a metallic thread. Remove the paper templates carefully, as they will be used again for quilting guides later in the assembly of this project. Do not trim the individual blades yet.

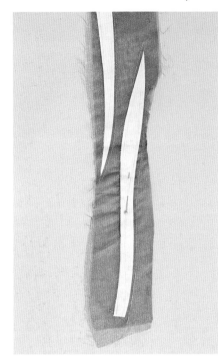

Press templates onto fused fabrics and outline stitch.

3. Because both sides of these blades of grass will be visible, it is necessary to work with decorative threads in both the top and the bobbin. Stitch straight lines up and down the blade of grass, inside the outline stitching. Place these lines very close together. You are actually "painting" this blade of grass with thread. Vary the thread colors on each leaf to add variety and realism. When you finish one line of stitching, turn over the fused fabric and work the next line of stitching from the other side. Using different shades in the bobbin, reversing sides, and occasionally changing thread colors will give variety to each leaf surface.

4. When you have completed thread painting the blades of grass, cut them out with very sharp scissors or a rotary cutter, carefully avoiding the stitching but cutting as close to the stitching as possible. Cut the bottom edge of the grass blade straight and clean.

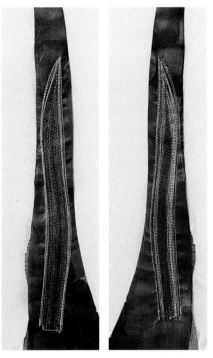

Stitch grass blade from both sides before trimming and treating with fray check.

5. Apply fray check to the entire length of the cut edge to prevent fraying or threads from coming undone at the bottom. Set aside to dry.

machine needle tip

When stitching through fused fabrics for an extended period of time, it helps your needle and thread to perform better if you occasionally unthread the machine and sew several lines through an alcohol wipe. The alcohol in the wipe will remove any built up gum from your needle and parts of the bobbin casing.

thread painting tip

Use some unexpected colors in your thread painting, as they give life to the natural colors. Note the purples in the finished sample photos.

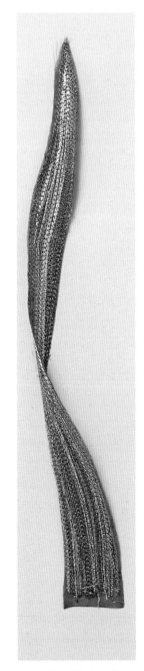

Set aside completed blades of grass to dry. Note the natural grasslike curl and variety of threads used.

Making the Dragonflies

The 3-D dragonflies are created with fused fabrics, but follow this section step by step, as organza requires special treatment with a relatively low iron temperature. For each dragonfly, two squares of organza are fused together, stamped, and decoratively stitched again. These 3-D dragonflies will be attached to the design last.

Instructions for Each Dragonfly

1. Preheat the iron to a low temperature. An iron that is too hot will wrinkle and melt organza. Test the temperature on a scrap of organza.

2. Place a piece of organza on the pressing cloth. Remove paper from one side of the lightweight fusible web and smooth the sticky side against the organza.

3. Press lightly. Let cool so that removing the paper doesn't remove the adhesive.

4. Remove the top paper from the lightweight fusible web. Place the second square of organza on top of the adhesive and press lightly between pressing cloths.

5. Pin the fused organza square to the foam core board.

6. Use a small flat paintbrush (or foam brush) to apply paint to the stamp, as you did in Step 2 of Fabric Stamping, page 60.

7. Stamp the organza. Hold the stamp down for a few seconds and then lift straight up.

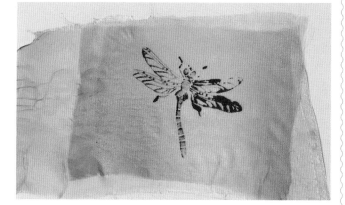

Fused and stamped organza

8. Let dry, then heat set using a dry iron set to a low temperature. Use pressing cloths to protect the iron and ironing board.

9. Using a free-motion foot, outline stitch the stamped dragonfly and stitch the lines in the wings with a variety of decorative threads.

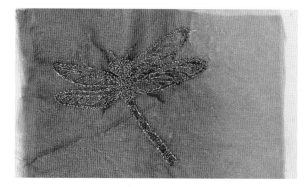

Stitched organza dragonfly

10. Cut out the dragonfly with very sharp scissors; set aside.

Cut out dragonfly.

Assembling the Parts

Because the dragonfly is such an ethereal and darting creature, I felt that a binding on this wallhanging would be too heavy and structured. Instead it is completed with a raw edge and a decorative top stitch. I added bead clusters here and there.

1. Trim each piece for layering. In the sample, the batting is ¼" bigger than the trimmed painted background all around. The backing fabric is approximately ¼" larger than the trimmed batting on the bottom and sides, but it is 2½" *longer at the top.* These choices are personal and are made based on the color frame formed by the batting. If you particularly like a part of your colored batting, this difference in size could be adjusted to allow more of it to show. The bottom edges were cut in freehand curves, each layer purposely not matched.

2. Prepare the backing fabric by folding the 2½″ at the top down against the wrong side of the fabric. Stitch the turned edge across the backing to create a sleeve for hanging.

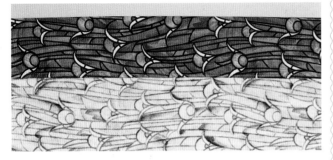

Fold backing toward inside to form hanging sleeve.

3. Run a line of fray check around the edge and set aside to dry.

Making the Sandwich

1. Lay the prepared backing fabric on a table, right side down, with the folded section facing up. Spray with adhesive (remember to do this in a well-ventilated area or outside).

2. Place the painted batting over the backing fabric. Smooth gently with your hands. Spray adhesive on the top side of the batting.

3. Lay the stamped and stitched piece on top of the batting, right side up. Gently smooth with your fingers to adhere the 3 layers together.

4. Use the freezer paper grass templates as a guideline for free-motion quilting by pressing them onto the design surface in a pleasing arrangement. Using a walking foot, quilt around these templates to duplicate the grasses blowing in the wind, being careful not to stitch through the dragonflies.

Quilt around grass blade templates.

5. Quilt around the outline of the stamped dragonfly. This will make him puff out a bit.

Adding the Grass

1. Arrange the grasses as if they were drifting in the wind, placing shorter blades in front of longer blades and twisting some stems once, while leaving others flat. Tack down the tip and centers of the blades to the background with a hidden hand stitch that does not go through to the backing. Add beads to this stitch if you wish.

2. Stitch the bottom edge of the blades of grass to the bottom of the wallhanging with a simple straight stitch and invisible thread. Decorative stitching and a sprinkle of beads will hide this stitching later.

Top Stitching the Edges

I used a metallic thread in the machine and a colored cotton thread in the bobbin to match the backing. Loosen the tension on the bobbin casing just a little so that a bit of bobbin thread pulls up to the top, giving the top-stitched line a two-color look. The stitch in this photo was set at a number 8 on my Pfaff.

Loosen bobbin thread so it will pull up to top.

1. With a walking foot topstitch across the top edge to edge, ¼″ from the top edge of the *painted* fabric (this is about 1″ from the top of the backing fabric). Backstitch at the start and finish to prevent unraveling (you are allowing for the hanging rod with this step).

2. Start a new line of top stitching ½″ down from the first one. Stitch in ¼″ from the edge of the painted fabric and stop with the needle down. Make a right angle turn, taking the stitching lengthwise down the wallhanging.

Start second line of topstitching ½″ from first line.

3. Continue topstitching ¼″ from the edge all the way down the right side, across the curved bottom, and up the left side, using the edge of the painted fabric as a guide. At ½″ from the top line, stop with the needle down, make a right angle turn toward the outside edge, and continue to the edge, backstitching before snipping the threads.

Embellishing

1. Add beads among the grasses and a few beads scattered randomly around the dragonflies.

2. Hand stitch the organza dragonflies over the stitched and quilted dragonfly outlines on the background. Place them slightly off center so that the image on the background appears to be a shadow. You may want to embellish the dragonfly with some beads.

Attach dragonflies to stamped and stitched design.

Hanging Rod

Use a branch or dowel inserted through the tube as a hanging rod for this little quilt. Add some fabric beads, page 24, to the sample as a final embellishment. I threaded the beads on decorative yarns and tied the yarns over the ends of the stick with a half hitch.

Add homemade fabric beads to ends of the hanging rod.

The Heron, 11½″ × 15½″ by Judy Bartel

bonus project: Ladybug ATC

Creating grass blades as a 3-D addition to your artwork can also be done on a smaller scale. Here is a little ATC done with the same technique.

Ladybug ATC, 2½″ × 3½″, by Judy Bartel, with blades of grass and button embellishment

Instructions

1. Prepare a background fabric using a 2½″ × 3½″ piece of painted fabric.

2. Use a leaf-themed rubber stamp to add stamped designs to the painted fabric. Set aside to dry.

3. Fuse together 2 pieces of organza 4″ × 5″.

4. Draw 4″-long blades of grass of varying widths on the fused organza or use freezer paper and the templates on page 61.

5. Topstitch the organza grass blades in various colors.

6. Cut out the grass blades close to the edge stitching. Use fray check to secure the edges.

7. Place the grass blades on the surface of the painted fabric. They can cross over each other for added depth. Trim the blades where they overlap the edges.

8. Sandwich your backing, Timtex, and surface-designed fabric. Finish with a satin stitch around the edges, catching the ends of the grass in the satin stitch.

9. Embellish with a button or bead representing an insect. You could do a ladybug, as shown, or perhaps a spider or a fly.

cherry tree in bloom
Journal Cover

Freeform stitching in an embroidery hoop, free-motion quilting, beading with sequins, adding embellishments to complement the theme, and a double-braid edge applied with the machine

Cherry Tree in Bloom journal cover, 8½″ × 11″

I was born and raised in the province of Alberta, Canada. It is the last toehold of the Rocky Mountains and stretches to the beginning of the prairies. It's very cold in winter and very dry in summer.

To live now in the Pacific rain forest is continually inspiring to me. I'll never forget the first time I went back to Alberta. The trees that seemed big when I left suddenly seemed the size I remembered as a child!

Because of the Pacific coast climate, I soon became a garden lover, most especially landscaping, with a love for trees. Marrying a logger has brought conflict. Where I want lots of big trees, he thinks he should be cutting everything down. So I present here a tree we can admire and never argue over pruning!

This tree is simple to make. When you first read the directions, you will probably think to yourself, "That won't work! It will snaggle up in the sewing machine." But not so. It's a wonderfully fun technique. I chose my background fabric first. This allowed me to select a thread color for the tree that enhanced the design. Then I chose my embellishments. Because I love double-flowering cherry trees, I went with an Asian fabric and embellishments.

Supplies

* **Background fabric, 8½˝ × 11˝ (You will need more if you are fussy cutting.)**
* **Muslin, 12˝ × 12˝**
* **Heavyweight stabilizer, 2 pieces 8½˝ × 11˝**
* **Threads to match background fabric and for stitching tree (I used Signature Variegated Machine Quilting Thread in the tree; for the shimmering highlights, I added Sulky Holoshimmer.)**
* **Chinese coins in 3 sizes, about 1¼˝, 1˝, ½˝ diameters**
* **Square bead, ¼˝ diameter**
* **Packet of tiny flower sequins**
* **2 packets of Delica beads in a color to match the sequins**
* **Decorative cord, 2 yards**
* **Jeans needle (100/16)**
* **Fray check**
* **Rotary cutter and acrylic ruler**
* **8˝ embroidery hoop (minimum size for this project)**
* **Grommets (optional)**
* **Awl (optional)**
* **Appliqué foot**
* **Free-motion foot**

Instructions

Thread Drawing the Tree

1. With a ruler and pencil, draw a 4˝ × 6˝ rectangle in the approximate center of the 12˝ × 12˝ muslin square.

2. Sew along the pencil line with a straight stitch and a short stitch length.

3. Cut away the center of the rectangle, leaving approximately ¼˝ inside the stay-stitch line.

4. Thread your machine with the thread for stitching the tree, using the same thread in the bobbin.

5. Mount the muslin in the hoop and stretch it firmly, taking care not to distort the rectangular hole. Cut away the excess outside the hoop to avoid extra fabric getting in the way. At the sewing machine, position the hooped muslin under the needle, with the short ends of the rectangle as the sides and the long edges as the top and bottom.

6. Start the needle behind the stay-stitch line and sew from the top to the approximate center on the opposite side of the rectangle. Stop with the needle in the down position. Lift the foot, turn the hoop, and stitch another line, aiming for a point at the top about ¼˝ away from the first line.

7. Repeat Step 6 over and over until you have a V shape. Use the muslin outside the stay-stitch line to anchor the line of stitching and to move to another area when necessary. It is OK to cross over the thread lines that will form the trunk area.

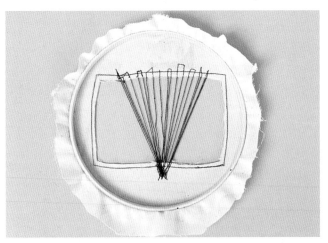

Begin V stitch lines for shadow tree.

8. With the basic V-shape formed, you are ready to form the trunk. With the needle down in the muslin at the bottom of the tree, set your machine to the widest zigzag stitch. Although this will pull together in a roll, setting the stitch wide will ensure that you have gathered all the strands into the trunk and it won't roll too tightly. Stitch from the roots to a point approximately 1″ up the thread lines. Stop with the needle down and change the stitch back to straight stitch.

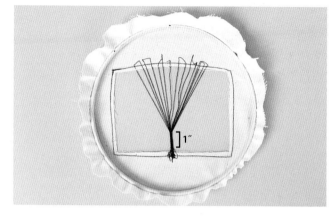

Complete trunk of tree.

Creating Major and Minor Branches

Now that the basic framework for the tree is done, you will be forming the shape of the upper tree. Have a good look at one of your favorite trees to study the actual proportion of the trunk, major and minor branches, and then the twigs.

1. Put the needle down at the top part of the trunk and set your machine to straight stitch. To form a major branch, straight stitch in one area back and forth about 10 times between the top of the tree trunk and the top edge of the muslin rectangle.

2. With the needle stopped in the down position on the trunk, change to your widest zigzag. Travel part way up this section of straight lines, gathering them into a major branch. Stop with the needle down; turn your work, stitching back down this part of the branch.

3. Repeat Steps 1 and 2, building major branches across the center section of the tree.

tree trunk tip

When the tree is complete, if you feel that the trunk needs widening, simply add lines of stitching up and down from the roots to the point where it branches. When the area is filled a bit, zigzag over these new threads, catching the side of the original trunk. Repeat this on the other side. This will also give the trunk a grooved and textured appearance.

Build the major branches.

stitching tip

Make sure to anchor each end of each line in either the tree stitching or the muslin border. This prevents them from tangling or bunching up.

safety tip

Use an awl or long pin to keep threads from one branch away from the others and to avoid sewing through your fingers.

4. When you zigzag to the end of a major branch and have reset your machine to a straight stitch, change the angle slightly and stitch back and forth between 2 branches 5 or 6 times to form a minor branch shape. Use the zigzag stitch to tack these branches together, thus making narrower minor branches. At this point, the lines are short enough that it isn't necessary to stop and turn. You can use forward and reverse stitch to form a minor branch, but *always* make sure that this stitch line is anchored in either a branch or trunk in the muslin at each end.

5. If you wish to add some sparkle, as in the sample, re-thread your machine with Sulky Holoshimmer. This gives the tree a shimmering reflection of light. Do a simple open zigzag stitch up and down one side of the trunk and some of the branches to add these highlights.

branch tip

Form the canopy of the tree by angling off from one branch to form another. As in a real tree, cross over some branches. Use the already formed branches and trunk to move about within your tree.

finishing tip

If you feel your tree is finished but aren't sure, take the hoop away from the machine. Lay the hooped muslin over a piece of white paper and draw in some more branches. This will indicate whether they add to the composition before actually stitching them. They may be unnecessary.

Completed tree in muslin frame (Stitching time for this tree is approximately 1 hour.)

Removing from Muslin

1. When you are satisfied with your tree, remove the muslin from the hoop.

2. Over a double layer of paper towels, use fray check to finish the branch tips and the roots. Touch the part that will be cut and give the bottle a gentle squeeze to saturate through all threads. Set aside to dry.

3. When the fray check is totally dry, cut away each branch just inside the muslin. Your tree is now ready to apply to a background.

Completed tree cut away from muslin

Preparing the Background

1. Spray a piece of 8½″ × 11″ heavyweight stabilizer with an adhesive or use a gluestick.

2. Place the chosen background fabric over the stabilizer and smooth it while pressing down. I iron mine at this point to make sure it's straight.

3. Free-motion quilt on the layered background. I simply outlined the fabric design, as it seemed to go with the theme. Stippling or any other design you like doing will work at this point.

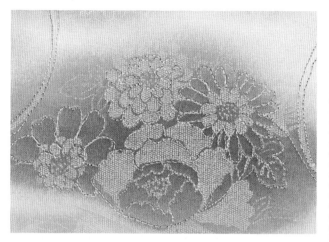

Quilt around print on background fabric.

Applying the Tree

1. Arrange the tree and other embellishments on the quilted background. When you find an arrangement you like, take a picture of it. Because you have to remove all the sequins and beads after pouring them out, it is nice to have it recorded for reference.

Play with arrangement of tree and other embellishments.

2. Stitch the tree to the background by hand with matching thread. Make small stitches by coming up from the back, going over a couple of threads, and returning down through the back. Work up the trunk and spot stitch here and there among the branches. These stitches should be invisible, as they are not part of the design.

Embellishments

Add the sequins by hand first. Bring a threaded needle up from the back, catching the tip or edge of a branch, and thread through a sequin and a Delica bead. Return the needle down through the sequin (going around the bead) and back down through the background. Continue in this way until your tree is in full bloom. Use a few at the bottom to cover where the trunk meets the ground.

sequin tip

Sequins can sometimes become static and are difficult to work with, as they stick to your bowl and your fingers. I use a lint roller to pick up a few sequins and a few beads, picking them off the sticky surface with the needle. This way not so many beads go in the vacuum cleaner! Waxing your thread can also help keep the static down.

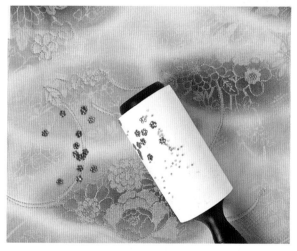

Use lint roller to tame runaway sequins and beads.

Finishing the Journal Cover

1. Sandwich another layer of heavyweight stabilizer between the backing fabric and the embellished top. After the layers are lined up perfectly and spray basted together, use an appliqué foot and a buttonhole stitch to bind the decorative cord to the edge, covering the layers. The stitch is applied *in mirror image* so that the straight stitch goes down the edge of the page and the outreaching stitches capture the cord. Use the same thread color in the bobbin and machine.

Apply cord to edge.

2. Repeat the stitching in Step 1 to lay a second length of cord right beside the *inner* edge of the first cord to completely frame the page.

3. Add Chinese coins by looping a length of decorative cord in half, feeding it through the hole, and tying a knot big enough to secure it in place. Thread the ends back through the hole to the back of the coin. Repeat with additional coins, spacing each at even intervals along the length.

Double knot through holes in Chinese coins.

4. Stitch the string of coins to the side of the journal page with thread that matches the cord. Take care to place the stitches neatly so that the stitches on the back do not detract from the appearance.

5. Loop the ends up and wrap them in place to form the double loop at the bottom.

6. Stitch the square bead in place over the wrapped cord.

Attach coin strand to journal page.

7. Attach the finished page to a journal with the method of your choice. It can be attached by lacing through holes created with an awl or through grommets, bound in a book-making fashion, or punched for rings.

– OR –

The page can also be used as a wallhanging. Make a small hanging sleeve on the back by forming a tube of fabric 7″ long and hemmed at each end. Press the tube so the seam is on the bottom side and hand stitch it to the top of the backing with an overhand stitch.

bonus project:
Shadow Tree ATC

By changing the size (or shape) of the area worked in the hoop, the tree can also become a great embellishment on a postcard or ATC.

Shadow Tree ATC, 2½″ × 3½″, by Judy Bartel

Instructions

1. For an ATC-sized project, cut a 2¾″ × 3¾″ rectangle in the center of a piece of muslin and large enough to put in your hoop. This gives you room to work a small tree, either vertically or horizontally.

2. Follow the same steps as described for the larger tree, page 68. When finished, treat with fray check, let dry, and cut free of the muslin.

3. For the background, prepare a 2½″ × 3½″ piece of hand-painted fabric laid over a piece of Timtex the same size. Secure these together using a gluestick.

4. Place the tree on top of the background and arranged as desired. Pin the tips into place.

5. Using a gluestick, secure the backing to the Timtex.

6. Satin stitch the edges with a wide stitch, catching the ends of each branch and the trunk.

Now you have a nice little ATC for your collection, to use at your next trading session, or as a gift for a friend.

Stone Arch, 4″ × 8¼″, with shadow tree, by Judy Bartel. This technique can be used on any size project. Judy added wool felting with her embellishing machine and used textured paints to simulate the stone arch.

the lady with the blues
Wallhanging

Computer printing on fabric, free-motion quilting, raw-edge appliqué, turning pieces right side out, beading and hand appliqué, wool yarns, and embellishments

technique that has been very popular with quilters in the recent past is using the computer and printer to add features to textile art. With the right equipment, this is not complicated and can be very rewarding.

The Lady with the Blues Wallhanging, 13½″ × 22½″

Supplies

* **Wood grain print batik for the main background, ½ yard**
* **Dyed mulberry bark, approximately 6″ × 6″**
* **Blue suedette fabric, ¼ yard**
* **Organza, ½ yard *each* of four colors (The sample has 3 blues and a rust in the hair.)**
* **Muslin, ½ yard**
* **Sparkly beige organza to cover face, 2 squares 5″ × 5″**
* **Very light wool batting, 5″ × 5″**
* **Batting, 14″ × 23″**
* **Backing fabric, 14″ × 23″**
* **Quilter's Freezer Paper**
* **Bubble Jet Set**
* **Large disposable container (I use the one salad mix comes in.)**
* **A collection of decorative yarns and threads in colors matching the hair (Oliver Twists, 2 packages)**

* **Beads, matching and highlighting hair colors**
* **Turning tools**
* **Computer**
* **Inkjet printer**
* **Crafter's heat gun**
* **Crayons—pink and blue**
* **Threads matching your fabric**
* **Fray check**
* **Straight pins**
* **Beading needle**
* **Embroidery floss to match mulberry bark**
* **Tea to tea-dye the muslin**
* **Large bowl**
* **Boiling water**
* **Free-motion foot**

Instructions

Treating the Muslin for Printing

First, you need to tea dye your muslin. This provides an aged look to the fabric for printing the text.

1. Put the muslin in a bowl large enough to submerge it all. Add 2 heaping tablespoons of loose tea and cover with boiling water. Set aside for ½ hour. Do not disturb during this time to give the fabric a subtle, uneven coloring. Remove, rinse, and press to dry.

2. To make the printout permanent, it is necessary to pretreat the tea-dyed fabric with Bubble Jet Set. Follow the manufacturer's directions.

3. Pour the remaining liquid back into the bottle. It can be used over and over. Although it does become slightly discolored, this has never affected any of my projects.

4. From the treated muslin, cut a 9″ × 12″ piece of tea-dyed muslin for the text.

Printing Text on Treated Fabric

1. Cut a piece of freezer paper 9″ × 12″. Press it onto one side of the tea-dyed and Bubble Jet Set-treated fabric.

2. Trim this fabric-paper piece to exactly 8½″ × 11″. Trimming at this stage gives the piece very clean edges to feed through the printer rollers.

3. Place your sheet of fabric in the paper tray of the printer, facing the proper direction for printing.

4. Open your word-processing program and type the text you want to use in this project. Format the typeface to be decorative *but* choose a clear print style. Print the text onto the fabric.

5. Remove the paper backing and heat set with a dry iron.

6. Cut an oval shape around the text. Place the oval on a flat surface that will resist heat, such as a cork tile. Hold it in place with a chopstick and use a heat gun to burn the edges and other areas, giving it an aged look. Be careful not to obliterate the printed text.

Have a cup of water on hand. If the cotton starts to glow and burn too fast, simply dip your finger in water and press on the edge to stop the burning.

Preparing the Face

1. Use a copy machine to enlarge the face template 200%. Cut a piece of tea-dyed muslin, 2 pieces of organza, and a piece of wool batting to the sizes indicated. The seam allowance is included on this template.

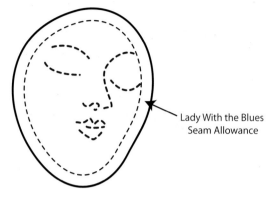

Lady With the Blues
Seam Allowance

Face template pattern—Copy at 200%.

2. Use the template and a pencil to trace the outline and features for the face onto the muslin. Make the lines dark enough to be visible through a layer of organza. These pencil lines will be covered later.

3. Make a slit in the middle of *one* oval of organza.

Layers for face

4. Place the batting on a work surface. Place the muslin oval on top of the batting, with the drawing facing up. Place the solid organza oval on top of the muslin and the slitted organza on top of that. Stitch the layers together, following the ¼″ seamline. Trim the seam to ⅛″.

Stitched layers for face

5. Turn the layered oval through the slit in the organza. The oval layers are as follows: organza with sketched muslin underneath, batting, and a backing of the slitted organza. Use a pressing cloth to protect the organza; use a low temperature iron setting to press the oval face flat.

6. Using suitable thread colors, stitch the facial details of the eyes, nose, and lips by hand or machine.

7. Rub the flat end of a pink wax crayon on the cheeks in a circular motion to give it some life. Do the same with the blue crayon on the eyelids. Set aside.

Cutting and Sewing the Hair

Wisps of hair are stitched on two layers of transparent organza, turned right side out, and then applied to the quilted backing with machine stitching. The stitching is then covered with beads and decorative wool. The open ends of the turned pieces are tucked under the side of the face.

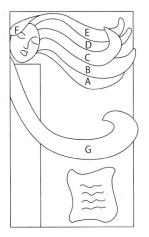

Design layout reference

1. Make a full-sized sketch for the layout of your lady, keeping in mind that my project is approximately 13" x 22". Use this design layout as a reference; your piece may vary in size—this is art and not an exact reproduction. Draw your own wisps of hair and the body wrap to fit your design and label each piece with a letter for final placement in your project. Then experiment with colors to fill in the layout; keep this for reference.

2. Use a copy machine to make several copies of your sketch so that you can cut a template for each piece. These copies can be black and white since you have letters on each piece. Trace onto freezer paper each template that you have cut.

sewing on bias tip

These swirling pieces of bias organza are more difficult to sew than if using cotton. This "difficulty" is also the reason that organza is used on the bias—it gives more flexibility! After these pieces are turned, they remain soft and flexible, so that you can easily flex them to lay where you want them in the design.

3. Cut 2 pieces of organza large enough to accommodate the freezer paper templates positioned diagonally on the fabric. Pin together the 2 layers of organza. Place the freezer paper templates *on the bias* of the transparent fabric and lightly press it to the fabrics, avoiding the pins. *Do not cut yet.*

4. Stitch just outside the edge of the templates with a small straight stitch, starting and ending at the dots. The fabric will unravel easily, so dab fray check *on* the stitch line and let dry before cutting. Press and cut out, leaving approximately ⅛" of seam allowance.

5. Use a turning tube to turn the pieces right side out (see Turned Pieces with Small Openings, page 15). Make sure the seams are turned out all the way and the shape is full.

6. Set the iron to a cool temperature so the organza will not melt. Cover the organza with a pressing cloth and press gently. Set aside.

Preparing the Background

1. Cut the background fabric to 14" × 24".

2. Layer together *only* the background fabric with the batting. Free-motion quilt along the wood grain lines in the print. Note that the backing fabric has not been included yet.

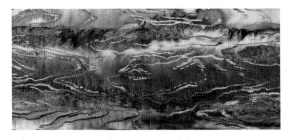

Quilt wood grain lines by following lines on print.

3. Cut a 2¾″ × 15″ strip of blue suedette. This rectangle will represent the body of the woman and will be appliquéd with a raw edge.

Finished pieces ready for assembly

Assembling

1. Place the quilted background on the work surface right side up.

2. Lay the blue suedette rectangular shape of the body on the left side of the background. Line up the edge of the rectangle with the outside and bottom edges of the background. Pin in place.

3. Straight stitch very close to the edge of the rectangle (about ⅛″) with matching thread. Satin stitch would work as well, especially if you have chosen a fabric that may fray. The sample is done with a double top stitch.

Adding the Face and Hair

1. Place the face at the top of the body rectangle. Do not pin or sew the face in place yet.

2. Arrange the hair around the face area, using the layout design for reference and allowing for the unfinished ends to be under the face. When you are satisfied with the arrangement of the hair and colors, pin everything in place. Before stitching, check to be sure all the hair is arranged so that the prepared face covers all the open ends of the hair strands—but *do not* pin the face in place yet. Remove the face from the design.

3. Refer to the design layout reference, page 77, and pin the body wrap (piece G) over the body and toward the

printed text (which will be added later). The left side of the wrap will be stitched into the side seam when the backing is added.

4. Stitch down the hair along the edges of each piece, using a small straight stitch in matching thread. Where the hair touches each other, stitch so that you catch both pieces. This stitching will be covered with decorative yarns later. Do not stitch the hair all the way to the edge along the right side of the design surface, as the hair and body wrap ends will be folded back from that edge to add the backing.

5. Keeping the ends free, place the prepared organza-muslin face at the top of the body rectangle. Pin in place, pinning *only along the outside edges. Do not pin in the middle of the face,* as doing so separates the threads in the organza. A slight tilt to the head will give her more emotion. Allow at least ¼″ from the edge for the backing seam.

6. Hand appliqué the quilted face in place over the raw ends of the hair. Lay decorative yarns along the stitching lines between the hair colors. Leave extra yarn length to extend beyond the fabric hair out into the background and some yarn to curl over the forehead and cheeks. These can be snipped off later if they are too long.

7. Tack down the pieces of yarn with a long, thin beading needle and thread that matches the yarns. *Play* during this step. Curl some over the face and tack it down. Make the hair look as if it is blowing away from the face in a wind, with the strands of wool looping beyond the organza pieces. Add beads and sparkly yarns until *you* are satisfied with the outcome. Again, remember that the embellishments along the edges will be folded away from the edges to add the backing and will be tacked down later.

Finishing the Quilt

1. Layer the finished top, right sides together, with the backing. Finish the quilt in the pillowcase style (see Pillowcase Finish, page 11). Care needs to be taken with all the organza hair pieces that extend beyond the edge of the quilt. Pin them toward the center and out of the way during this step. Sew down the right side, across the bottom, up the left side, and across the top, leaving an opening behind the hair that sweeps off to the right side for turning. This way, the hand stitching that closes this opening will be hidden behind the extended hair.

2. Clip the corners and turn the quilt right side out. Stitch the opening closed. Press lightly from the back, with the face and hair lying on a fluffy clean towel so that they don't get flattened. Add a few more beads in the hair to tack the layers together and to keep the quilt from sagging.

3. A hanging sleeve can be added to the back.

Adding the Text

1. Shape the mulberry bark frame by spritzing it with water until it is damp. Arrange the damp bark on a board or folded towel and pin into place. When it is dry, it will retain that shape.

2. Hand stitch the prepared tea-dyed text piece to the dry mulberry bark with a running stitch. Use embroidery thread in a suitable color—it is meant to look primitive.

3. Check the layout diagram for placement. Attach the bark-text piece to the quilt with hidden stitches through the 4 corners to tack the layers together.

bonus project: Computer-Printed ATCs

I have five glorious granddaughters and cherish each one of them. I think they are the most beautiful children on the face of the earth. But you know when you say to someone, "Do you want to see pictures of my grandchildren?" and their eyes glaze over? Well I've done these cards because when I pull **them** out, the person's interest is revived, both in how the pictures are presented **and** in my granddaughters!

Photos were printed on fabric with the computer and embellished with items representing each grandchild.

Supplies

* **Background fabric, 2½″ × 3½″ for each card**
* **Backing fabric, 2½″ × 3½″ for each card**
* **Timtex, 2½″ × 3½″ for each card**
* **Pre-treated printable fabric sheet (Printed Treasures)**
* **Threads, beads, baubles for embellishment and finishing**

Instructions

1. Use a computer software program of your choice to arrange your favorite photos in a layout that will allow for cutting the photos apart without losing any of the image. Print them on a pre-treated printable fabric sheet.

2. Remove the paper backing and cut the pictures apart. Trim the photos down to just silhouettes.

3. For each card, glue the surface fabric to the Timtex and place the picture as desired. Use a straight stitch around the photo to attach it to the background (raw edge appliqué). Add embellishment items that suit each child's photo.

4. Glue a 2½″ × 3½″ fabric piece to the back of the card. Finish the edges according to your preference.

leaf vine
Luggage Tags

Stamping on fabric, thread painting on soluble stabilizer, simple beading, and adding a fringe of woolen yarns.

3" × 6"

Luggage tags

3" × 7"

I like to use this technique to create my own embellishments. I learned to do this while working through Patti Medaris Culea's tome patterns. When I've created a project that needs a vine of leaves or a flower or anything else for which I would prefer not to use mass-manufactured embellishments, this is the method I choose. I love it. (Have you guessed yet that I love doing *all* this stuff?) I've added frogs to ponds, women to a beach, and vines on rock walls, all using this technique.

Let's start with something simple—a thread-painted vine. I've provided a pattern for you to trace. With this easy design, you can get the feel of working on soluble stabilizer before you start your own original design.

Supplies

Thread-Painted Vine

* 8″ embroidery hoop
* Vine drawing to trace
* Fine permanent marker
* Soluble plastic film stabilizer, 2 squares, 10″ × 10″
* Gold metallic thread in machine and bobbin
* Free-motion foot
* Bowl

Inchie

* Heavy-duty stabilizer, 1¼″ × 1¼″ square
* Rubber stamp, roughly 1″ × 1″
* Stamp pad ink
* Hand-painted fabric, 6″ × 6″

Luggage Tag

* Hand-painted fabric, 1 fat quarter (2 fat quarters if you want the back different from the front)
* Backing, 3″ × 6″
* Heavyweight stabilizer, 3″ × 6″
* Pinking shears
* Awl, heavy bodkin, or any tool you can use to punch a small hole through all layers
* Small grommet, optional (These are available in scrapbooking supply stores or your local quilt or craft shop.)
* 12 strands of 6 different decorative wools and threads
* Free-motion foot
* Strong thread or dental floss

Leaf vine pattern—Copy at 100%.

Instructions

Creating the Vine

1. With a permanent marker, trace the leaf vine pattern, above, onto a 10″ × 10″ square of soluble plastic stabilizer. Layer this with the second stabilizer square and place the sandwich in an embroidery hoop for stitching. You'll see some leaves that are not attached to the vine; you will be stitching those separate leaves to be used in the embellishing.

Trace pattern on soluble stabilizer and place in hoop for stitching.

plastic film tip

Using soluble plastic film designed for backing machine embroidery, rather than the clothlike film, will give you the best results. This product will wash away completely, whereas the clothlike film tends to leave bits of white that you cannot remove from this type of freeform work.

2. Thread your machine and bobbin with gold metallic thread. Use a free-motion foot and lower the feed dogs. This stitching *can* be done with regular thread, but I like metallic because it gives the leaves some body, allowing them to be bent and curled, which adds to the design.

3. To outline the design, start at the top of the stem, sew through the stabilizer down the stem, back up to the first branch, down that branch, around the leaf, and back to the main stem. Repeat this step to outline all of the design.

4. Use the main stem to travel from branch to branch, widening the vine and branches with stitch lines and filling in leaves. *Always make sure every stitch line connects with another stitch line, as this will hold the design together when it is soaked in water.* Fill each leaf. Stitch a vein line up the center of each leaf and return up its stem to the branch. Travel along the branch to the next leaf.

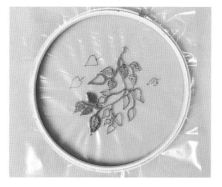

Outline stitch design (Sample done in different colors for illustration purposes.)

5. Proceed in this manner until all the leaves have been filled in. By now, there will be several stitch lines on each stem, branch, and along the center vine.

6. Set your machine to a medium zigzag and stitch down and back up each branch, stem, and main center stem. Refer to the illustration below to see how the zigzag will cover the lines of stitching.

Stitching stems

leaf stitching steps

1. Starting at the stem, stitch around the leaf's outline and continue with decreasing concentric shapes toward the leaf center. Head back up to the stem when done.

2. Travel down from the stem again, all the way to the leaf tip. Inside the leaf edges, stitch straight lines from side to side, crossing over the outlines made in Step 1 and stopping where the base of the leaf meets the stem.

3. At the stem, stitch downward from the center vein to the outside edge and slightly over (locking it all together), and then return back to the vein. Repeat this on the other side. Travel down the center vein a few stitches and repeat this vein line from the center to the outside edge. Do this 3 or 4 times per leaf, depending on its size.

4. Starting and ending at the point where the base of the leaf meets the stem, do a light, close zigzag stitch around the leaf's outside edge to make the edge a bit thicker.

5. From where the base of the leaf meets the stem, stitch a straight stitch to the point of the leaf and back up again at least 2 times. On the last trip up the center of the leaf, go all the way to the tip of the stem to define a center vein for the leaf.

Leaf stitching steps

7. Remove the stabilizer from the hoop. Trim off any loose threads. This piece will not unravel, as it has been "back-stitched" *a lot*!

Remove from hoop and trim loose threads.

8. Run lukewarm water in a bowl and immerse your stitching into the water. Let it soak a few minutes. The stabilizer dissolves very quickly, and the result is so rewarding. Your vine and the few separate leaves are now ready to use to adorn your luggage tag. Set aside to dry while you prepare the other elements.

Completed vine after soaking and drying

Making the *Inchie*

This simple tiny addition gives your luggage tag character. I used hand-painted fabric but in a different color for contrast.

1. Ink the rubber stamp and place the design on the 6″ × 6″ square of fabric. Stamp the design several times on the same piece of fabric. Trim the best stamp to a 1¼″ × 1¼″ square. Cut an unprinted 1¼″ × 1¼″ square from the 6″ × 6″ square of fabric for the backing.

2. Press the stamped square with a hot dry iron to set the ink.

3. Sandwich the 1¼″ × 1¼″ square of backing, the 1¼″ × 1¼″ square of heavyweight stabilizer, and the stamped square. Topstitch a line around the sandwich ¼″ from the edge with metallic thread.

4. Trim the edge with pinking shears, close to the stitching, and set aside.

Completed *Inchie*

Preparing the Tag for Embellishment

1. Cut the top fabric and heavyweight stabilizer to 3″ × 6″. Refer to the template to taper the upper corners. Use a gluestick or spray adhesive and finger-press the 2 layers together.

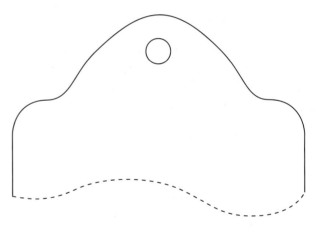

Tag top template—Copy at 100%. Taper upper corners of tag.

2. Place the finished *Inchie* somewhere in the top ⅓ of the tag. Attach by hand stitching through from the back and coming up in a corner. Add a bead to the thread and go back through to the underside. Attach all 4 corners in this way. Knot the thread on the back of the tag.

3. Place the stitched metallic leaf vine on the tag surface, arranging it in a pleasing layout. Pin in place.

4. Attach the vine to the tag with single stitches through all layers. Add beads to the anchoring stitches and perhaps a cluster here and there for added sparkle, similar to Step 2.

Add beads to anchoring stitches.

Sandwiching the Tag

1. Cut a 3″ × 6″ piece of fabric for the backing. If you want to write on or sign the backing of your tag, do it now, while it is still flat. For the sample, I used a rubber stamp with an art quote. Heat set the writing or stamped design.

2. Adhere the embellished layers of the luggage tag to the prepared backing fabric with spray adhesive or a gluestick. Smooth and finger-press together.

3. With the gold thread in your machine and bobbin, top stitch around the outside of the tag, approximately ¼″ from the edge, fastening the 3 layers together. Backstitch at the end of this top-stitched line. Snip threads.

4. Trim the edges of the tag with pinking shears.

Trim edges of tag with pinking shears.

Finishing

1. Use an awl or heavy bodkin to make a hole at the top of the tag. The hole should be big enough to put decorative yarns and threads through in a half hitch. You can insert a grommet into this hole or line the hole with a buttonhole stitch. Or, because it won't take a lot of wear and won't show when the decorative yarn is threaded through, you can use the hole as it is and just seal it with fray check.

2. Fold the lengths of yarn in half, keeping the loop open.

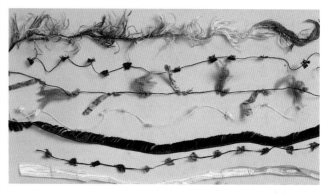

Strands of decorative yarn used in fringe

3. Thread a length of strong thread (or dental floss) through the folded loop of the yarn strands. Align the ends of the strong thread and use them as a threader to pull the loops of yarn through the hole in the tag. Pull all the loose yarn ends through the main loop and tighten up each strand to form a nice neat half hitch at the top of the tag. Remove the strong thread.

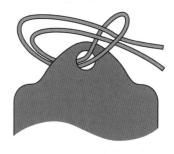

Half hitch knot

A piece of dental floss is an excellent thread for pulling your yarns through the tag hole. It's strong and easy to thread through the hole.

4. Select 2 or 3 strands of decorative yarns that have been pulled through the tag. Spread the rest back and out of the way. About ⅓ of the way up a strand, lay a single loose leaf (these are the separate leaves from your soluble stabilizer design). Machine zigzag stitch a line to the center of the leaf, catching the single strand of yarn. Do the same with the other single leaves, alternating their placement in the fringe.

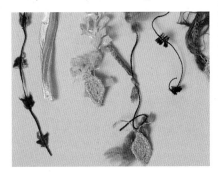

Attach single leaves to individual threads in fringe.

Now your luggage tag is done. Do you think you'll ever put it on your luggage?

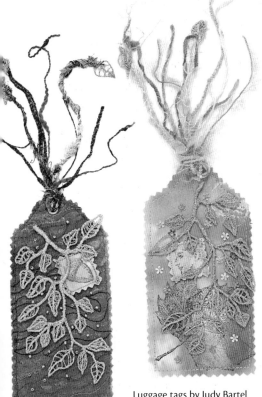

Luggage tags by Judy Bartel

bonus project: Leaf Sprig ATC

This little ATC is made with scraps of background cut from another quilt I was working on. It has curved piecing and twin-needle top stitching.

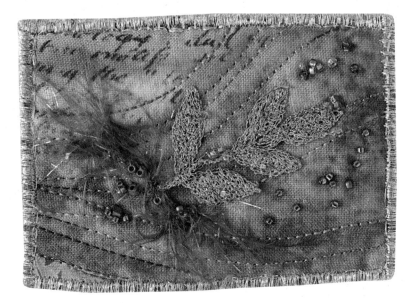

Leaf Sprig ATC, 2½″ × 3½″

Instructions

1. This project was made from the discarded pieces trimmed from the quilt *My Shadow*, page 94. The quilt was a curved piecing background that had been twin-needle topstitched. I saved the trimmings after cutting my quilt to size. To duplicate this card, use the curved piecing technique (see Cutting and Piecing Curved Seams, page 12) to create the background. When you apply the twin-needle stitching (see Twin-Needle Top Stitching, page 13), remember that the piece will shrink; so make the pieced background at least 4″ × 5″. Layer the background with some quilt batting and add some twin-needle stitching lines in waves across the surface. Trim to 2½″ × 3½″ for the ATC.

2. Make a little sprig of leaves by stitching gold metallic thread on soluble stabilizer and only doing a portion of the vine design (see vine pattern, page 80).

3. Soak the stitched stabilized vine in warm water until the stabilizer is dissolved. Allow the vine to dry, apply it to the ATC surface with a few gold beads, and attach 1½″ of fuzzy wool or yarn embellishment.

4. Use the computer to print a message onto the 2½″ × 3½″ backing fabric.

5. Apply the backing fabric and finish the edges with a satin stitch in metallic thread.

I added this project to give you a hint of an idea how my studio looks. **Everything** is too useful to throw away!

blossoms a la
Mucha Collage

Exploring collage and raw-edge appliqué, fabric selection, fussy cutting, and raw-edge appliqué

Close-up of face, hair, and body

Blossoms a la Mucha collage, 34″ × 40″

Collage is really fun to do. But I must warn you that if you have the least bit of a collecting streak, you are in trouble if you enjoy this technique. The best way to describe collage is to say it is a series of seemingly unrelated items or images that are gathered together to make a new whole.

A perfect example of inspiration and how it can affect your work is this chapter itself. When planning this chapter for the book, it was going to be a nature theme. I keep my fabrics on shelves sorted by color family, with the exception of my florals, rocks, woods, and ethnic supplies. When I set out to do this project, I went for the pile of leaf print fabrics, because my initial idea was a forest scene. But as sometimes happens, a totally unrelated piece of fabric was in that pile, and I was suddenly inspired to do something that reflected the art nouveau style of **that** piece of fabric. After all, it must have been misfiled for a reason!

This fabric inspired the project collage.

And with that, off I went on a completely different path. I stuffed that pile of leaf prints back on the shelf and went for the bin of florals. I had lots that would be good and decided this was it. So out came a big piece of paper, and a rough sketch was made approximately the size I wanted—and I do mean rough. For collage, it's best not to restrict yourself too much, as sometimes the images or pieces you wish to incorporate will not fit in the lines. It is better to be flexible with this technique.

Supplies

Fabric amounts will vary with the design of your own project.

* **Floral prints, variety of 10 to 12 pieces, ¼ yard each**
* **Background fabric, ¾ yard**
* **Border fabric, ¾ yard**
* **Backing fabric, ¾ yard**
* **Very fine black tulle, ¾ yard**
* **Batting, amount will vary with your finished design size**
* **Inspirational picture and sketching paper**
* **Chalk pencil**
* **Tea towel to protect pressing surface**
* **Scissors, very sharp**
* **Spray starch**
* **Spray adhesive**
* **Decorative yarns for hair**
* **Threads, variety of colors and types, including metallics**
* **Free-motion foot**
* **Lightbox or bright window**

Instructions

1. Draw a rough sketch of your inspirational image on paper. From this sketch, determine the appropriate size for your background piece; cut the piece.

My rough sketch

design sketch tip

The sketch is only necessary if you wish to make a picture that is representing an actual item. Collage can be abstract as well. Collage can also be done by simply cutting out all kinds of prints or portions of prints and then laying them out in an arrangement that suits you.

2. Pull out all the fabrics that are suitable for your project and spread them out on the work surface. Select the motifs you would like to see in your collage. To give you an idea of how a collage is laid out, I have provided a photograph of the fabrics used in this panel. I suggest that you play the game of "I Spy" or "Where's Waldo?" with them. Look at the fabrics used and see if you can find the motifs from them in the collage. In this way, you will learn how easy it is to combine a number of fabrics to create one image and how many different ways you can use each fabric.

Fabrics used in project collage panel.

3. Roughly cut out the motif you are going to use and lay it on your sketch as a beginning. Continue cutting pieces and motifs to fill in the design feature areas. It is impossible to provide an actual pattern for the panel featured here, as it is completely and totally dependent on what is in your stash. This particular collage was worked with a selection of floral fabrics, some light tan-colored pieces to give the idea of her stance, some wool for the hair, and a piece of satin for her dress, which is practically hidden.

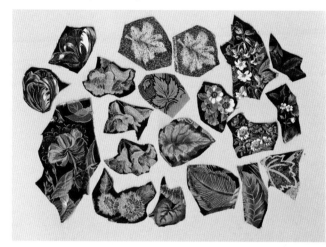

Roughly cut motifs for initial design layout.

4. Lay out the rough-cut pieces on your sketch to design your collage. Take a digital photograph of your layout when you are happy with it. You will use this photograph as a reference when laying down the fabrics.

Take snapshot of layout.

5. Cover the pressing surface with a tea towel. Spread out the cut motifs and saturate each piece with spray starch.

6. Press with a very hot dry iron.

7. Use a *very* sharp pair of scissors to fussy cut each motif as you wish to use it in the design. You will note that I have used the same motif in a couple of places, sometimes with a leaf attached and sometimes without.

Fussy cut motifs.

8. Tape your sketch to a window with bright light behind it or to a lightbox if you have one.

9. Place the background fabric over the sketch. Lightly trace the outlines of the sketch onto the background fabric using a chalk pencil.

10. Take the background piece off the window and lay it flat. Apply a very light touch of spray adhesive in the central area of the design, avoiding any areas that will show. Arrange your clipped motifs to fit within your sketch. You may discover (as I did) that you want your design to spill beyond the background area. You can add borders to the central background piece to accommodate the extension of the design. Handle the unit gently so the motifs that you have placed will remain in place. Use spray adhesive as necessary to continue arranging your clipped motifs on the bordered background.

spray starch tip

Some people advocate the use of fusible webbing at this stage and then press the motif down so that it's there for good. I prefer to work with just-stiffened fabric and a more forgiving spray adhesive. The starch keeps the cut edge crisp, and the spray adhesive allows me freedom to move motifs around while stitching. I have been known to change my mind and undo a bit of stitching to lift an edge and rearrange over or under the piece next to it. In this panel, I did that with the figure's feet.

11. Add the strands of decorative yarns for the hair. Simply place the yarn on the background and add a few pins if needed. Arrange the hair strand by strand until it looks pleasing with the rest of the design. The hair in this particular sample is a very fluffy soft yarn. Do a few anchoring stitches to hold the hair in place for now.

12. When you are happy with the layout, iron a piece of very fine black tulle the dimensions plus 1" of your background fabric (include the borders, if you added any)—enough tulle to completely cover your design surface. Layer the tulle over your design piece. The tulle will be sewn into the seams when you add the next border. Pin the tulle in place in several areas throughout the design.

tulle color tip

You can audition different tulle colors over your collage. I have found that black intensifies the colors, whereas white may wash them out. This is a matter of personal taste, so experiment to discover what you like.

13. Use your machine's free-motion foot to stitch with various colors of threads around the edges of the motifs. This is known as raw-edge appliqué (page 16), in which you perform the function of appliqué without turning under the edges. The black tulle over the design virtually becomes invisible, while at the same time prevents edges from fraying as the piece is handled.

tulle tip

Do be careful while stitching. The fine tulle can easily tear on a pin. Should this happen, consider whether a motif added to the surface will correct the situation. Sometimes this sort of action makes an error serendipitous. (Don't you just love that word? Such a pretty word to describe a mistake that ends up as a design element!)

14. Continue with free-motion stitching, changing colors to match or accentuate the area you are working on. I combined suitable colors and some metallic threads.

Free-motion stitching with a variety of threads

15. When everything is stitched into place, attach border strips, measured to fit the sides. Then attach the top and bottom borders, catching the edge of the tulle in the seams. This fastens down the tulle and offers permanent protection for the raw edges. You can add additional complementary borders as I did. Look at my project photo and notice that the inside red border is wider on the bottom than the sides and top. Be creative as you plan your borders.

Attach borders to tulle-covered center.

Quilting

This panel is shown *unquilted* so you can clearly see the stitching that was done to hold down the fabric pieces and to embellish them. Quilting is at your own discretion—as much or as little as you like.

Today's world of scrapbooking utilizes the art of collage for a lot of work. The little ATCs in Ephemera from Everywhere, page 17, are actually collages created from unmatched items that came together as a new creative whole.

Another great example of fabric collage is *Alert Bay Circa 1940*, page 92. The artist, Ionne McCauley, used a tree print as the perfect backdrop to her scene, with several other fabrics cut to represent buildings and logs. This quilt also employed raw-edge appliqué.

Collage-style ATC, 2½″ × 3½″, by Jan Hayman. Notice the piece of bamboo and little panda bear motifs cut and rearranged on background to create a new image.

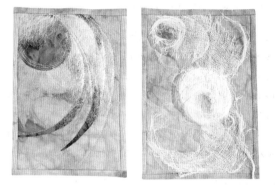

Two small panels by Sharon Pederson, 5″ × 7″, who used bits of metallic threads, cheesecloth, snippets of fabrics, and machine stitching to create a beautiful cosmic image out of seemingly unrelated elements

This collage project I made is a good example of how motif fabrics can be combined to create a completely different image.

Gallery
from small to wall

Hosta—Dream Queen, 12″ × 12″, designed and stitched by Diane Boyko. Diane's work with leaves is always stunning. This hosta leaf was created using pieced and turned leaves, twin-needle background texture, thread painting, and bead embellishment.

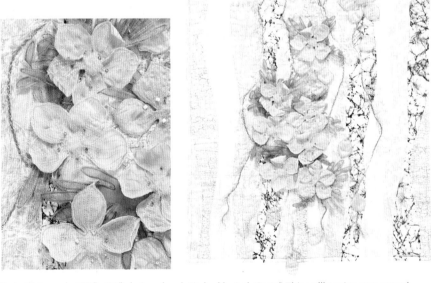

Spring Dogwoods, 17½″ × 21″, designed and stitched by Judy Bartel. This wallhanging uses curved piecing in the background, twin-needle topstitching, fused organza flowers, and bead embellishment.

With a Little Help from My Friends, 18½″ × 21″, designed and stitched by Donna Pepper. This is an excellent example of using the small techniques to make small projects and then combining them all for a larger wall-hanging. Donna made a series of little cards much like ATCs, mounted them on a quilted background, and used theme-related embellishments.

Donna had a stroke several years ago and was left without the use of one hand. Despite this disability, she has remained involved and enthusiastic in her textile art. When asked if I could mention her working with only one hand, her response was, "If it encourages one other person to keep trying, I will be happy."

Donna chose the African theme because African women today depend greatly on help from their friends. She tells us she also depends on her friends to continue encouraging her and offering an extra hand once in a while.

Ginkgo on My Mind, 24″ × 32″, designed and stitched by Gladys Love. This wall-hanging uses twin-needle topstitching, pieced and turned leaves, and computer-printed fabric. It is embellished with seed beads, silk rods, and silk cocoons.

Alert Bay Circa 1910, 16¾″ × 28½″, designed and stitched by Ionne McCauley. This is Ionne's version of what this area on the Vancouver Island coast looked like a long time ago. The longhouse had a raven painted on the front (done here with thread painting), and the pole on the front of the house had a large raven's beak on it. Part of the beak dropped down to reveal a ceremonial door.

The incredible machine quilting in the borders represents the carving on the pole. Techniques used in this quilt are thread painting and raw-edge appliqué, but no fusing. The picture is made separately and sewn onto a strip-pieced background. The background fabrics were chosen to extend and darken the colors and values used in the picture. The fabrics used for the background were Ionne's own hand dyes.

Close-up of Native art design quilting and thread painting on longhouse

Close-up of quilting done by Ionne McCauley

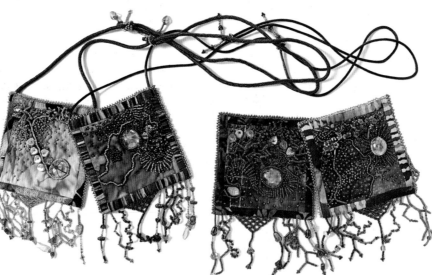

Beaded Amulet Bags, 4″ × 4″, designed and stitched by Eileen Neill. Eileen is a master bead worker extraordinaire. Her work is always awe inspiring. These amulet bags are made with little 4″ quilt surfaces that are heavily embellished and then turned into a pocket necklace. The cord is adjustable to hang any length. These bags are wonderful for keeping your cell phone with you wherever you go.

Alien Pop Can, 4″ × 6″, designed and stitched by Judy Bartel. This postcard is made with a squashed pop can found on the beach. I thought it looked like an alien and challenged my friend Judy to use it in some way. Judy met that challenge extremely well, using paint, embossing powder, and felting, all of which are techniques in this book. The swirls that look like planets are hot glue that has cooled and then been painted and embossed.

Fantasy Fishes, 41″ × 20″, designed and stitched by Flo Peel. This is a phenomenal piece that features appliqué, a pieced background, and some incredible beading. Flo's quilt was juried into Canada's annual Grand National Quilt Show in Kingston, Ontario, where last year's theme was Fantasy.

Ruby Notecard, 4″ × 6″, designed and stitched by Eileen Neill. Here is a unique layering technique using collage and embellishments to create a paper card. Eileen has created a little card using silk-waste yarn to form the shape of the doll and then overlaid it with tulle. She then free-motion stitched around it to contain the yarn and draw the shape. This card was then mounted on a background and then to the paper card. Isn't it wonderful?

Close-up of turned hair pieces and embellishments in *My Shadow*

My Shadow, 36" × 42", designed and stitched by Gladys Love. This quilt was inspired by the photo I took of my own shadow on a garden path. It was juried into the Grand National Quilt Show in Kingston, Ontario. The quilt employs curved piecing, twin-needle top stitching, machine appliqué, and turned and embellished hair pieces.

Shadow Tree ATC pocket page. This 5" × 7" pocket page is designed for ATCs. Created for me in a round robin exchange by Penny Crompton of Australia, this page employs the shadow tree methods with leaf-shaped bead embellishments. The pocket at the bottom is formed by straight stitching in colored threads on tulle.

Resources

Barbara Willis Stuffing Forks
www.barbarawillisdesigns.com
415 Palo Alto Avenue
Mountain View, CA 94041

Bella Nonna Design Studio
Silk petals
www.bellanonnaquilt.com

Eileen's Studio
Beads and sequins
235 Crescent Road West
Qualicum Beach, BC
Canada V9K 1J9

Huckleberry's
Fabrics, stabilizers, needles, thread
1930 Ryan Road East
Comox, BC
Canada V9M 4C9

Joggles
Turning tubes, hemostats, rubber
stamps
www.joggles.com
(mail order only)

Louise Jackson
Mostly Silk
Dupioni silks, suedette
745 E. 55th Avenue
Vancouver, BC
Canada V5X 1N8

Patti Medaris Culea
Creative cloth doll faces and
rubber stamps
www.pmcdesigns.com
9019 Stargaze Avenue
San Diego, CA 92129

Pebeo Inc.
Fabric paints
1905 Rue Roy
Sherbrooke, Quebec
Canada J1K 2X5

Janet Finch
Sew Can You
Threads
2505 14th Avenue
Port Alberni, BC
Canada V9Y 2X8

Stitches Quilt Shop
Fabric paints, silks, organzas
www.stitchesquiltshop.com
127 Rainbow Road
Salt Spring Island, BC
Canada, V8K 2V5

The Stamping Ground
Laurie Kanester
Box 385
Shawnigan Lake, BC
Canada V0R 2W0

Treenway Silks
Mulberry bark, silk rods, cocoons
www.treenwaysilks.com
501 Musgrave Road
Salt Spring Island, BC
Canada V8K 1V5

Kitambaa Designs
www.pippamoore.ca

Reference Books
Altered Photo Artistry, Beth
Wheeler and Lori Marquette

Beaded Embellishment, Amy C.
Clarke and Robin Atkins

Creative Cloth Doll Faces, Patti
Medaris Culea

Cutting Curves from Straight Pieces,
Debbie Bowles

Elegant Stitches, Judith Baker
Montano

Skydyes, Mickey Lawler

Photo by Don Emerson.

About the Author

Gladys Love is an assistant to the administrators at a senior high school. Her work consists largely of data entry and computer-generated reports. Her art is an antithesis to the rigid and organized demands of her work, giving her an outlet for her creativity and her love of textiles. With this book, she has been allowed to share some of her favorite techniques and designs. Gladys lives among the ocean, mountain, and forest grandeur of Vancouver Island with her husband, *his* dog, and a cat.

Great Titles *from* C&T PUBLISHING

Available at your local retailer or **www.ctpub.com** *or* **800.284.1114**

For a list of other fine books from C&T Publishing,
ask for a free catalog:

C&T PUBLISHING, INC.

P.O. Box 1456

Lafayette, CA 94549 | Email: ctinfo@ctpub.com

(800) 284-1114 | Website: www.ctpub.com

C&T Publishing's professional photography services are now
available to the public. Visit us at www.ctmediaservices.com.

For quilting supplies:

COTTON PATCH

1025 Brown Ave.

Lafayette, CA 94549

Store: (925) 284-1177 | Email: CottonPa@aol.com

Mail order: (925) 283-7883 | Website: www.quiltusa.com

Note: Fabrics used in the quilts shown may not be
currently available, as fabric manufacturers keep
most fabrics in print for only a short time.